Practical Sales Forecasting

Practical
Sales Forecasting

William Copulsky

American Management Association, Inc.

Standard book number: 8144–2132–6
Library of Congress catalog card number: 75–104100

Contents

I

Forecasting
and the Forecaster

THE July 12, 1965, issue of *Chemical & Engineering News* ran a special report entitled "Business Forecasting: Uncertain, Imprecise, Unavoidable." This title strikes a proper keynote for the subject of forecasting—or perhaps this quote from Dante's *Inferno* would be more appropriate: "Abandon all hope, you who enter here." In examining the goals and methods of this "uncertain, imprecise, unavoidable" part of business planning, this book will attempt to add an appreciable amount of certainty and precision to the process.

The Areas of Business Forecasting

In the typical large company, business forecasting is used primarily in three main areas:

- Financial budgeting.
- Strategic planning.
- Research planning.

Financial budgeting. Financial budgeting is generally centered around a detailed five-year budget. About November of each year, each operating unit is expected to furnish a financial budget for the following five years, covering the principal income, expense, and balance sheet items: sales, costs, profits, capital expenses, and flow of funds. The greatest detail is given for the forthcoming year; less detail is shown for the following four-year period. In addition to these detailed quantitative figures, which are broken down for major product groups and lines, qualitative material outlining the future plan of the operating unit is included to assist top management in analyzing the figures. These data are then assembled and coordinated by the parent company's financial group, and presented to top corporate management.

Strategic planning. To some extent, strategic planning is incorporated into the qualitative information that accompanies the five-year budget. Since the outline of a company's actions is basically a statement of intentions that assumes certain facts about the future environment in which the company will operate, any such outline is dependent upon forecasting. In order for a company treasurer to come up with five years' worth of financial calculations, company management must have some idea of how the company will grow—through new plants, new products, research and development, and acquisitions. In addition, the company must make periodic planning studies of areas in which it is heavily engaged.

Research planning. While much of every company's research is devoted to short-term problems, breakthroughs in potentially large-volume products usually come from longer-term research. The research planner must think in terms of more than five years ahead, because it may take that long to take his research from the laboratory to the first commercial plant. He must be guided by his evaluation not only of future markets but also of future technology. He must have clues not only about market size but also about the kind of competition that he will face from technical innovation.

Take the case of a company involved in nuclear energy. Here is a brief list of some of the comparative economic and technical factors that must guide research planning:

    A. Economic factors.
        1. Long-range energy needs of the world.
        2. Economics of nuclear reactions versus fossil fuel as energy sources.
    B. Technical factors.
        1. Changing efficiency of reactors.
        2. Changing requirements of fission reactors—uranium versus thorium as fuel.
        3. Timing of replacement of fission (present uranium-splitting type) reactors by fusion (hydrogen-bomb type) reactors.

Because investment commitments in nuclear energy are huge, and because research is introducing rapid changes, the research planner has to look far ahead, perhaps as far as the year 2000. How accurate will he be? Perhaps plus or minus 50 percent, but any estimate is better than no estimate, and to be 50 percent right is better than to be 100 percent wrong.

The Reasons for Forecasting

Man has always been curious about the future, but sheer curiosity is not the only reason for forecasting. In the three main planning areas that we have just described, forecasts have many uses. For example, in financial budgeting, forecasts set up standards by which management can judge its own performance independent of external factors not under its control. Forecasts also enable proper scheduling of plant and facility expansions, which often take at least one or two years, and sometimes five or more. By using forecasts, management can think ahead on needs for more capital, and can schedule borrowings or float stock issues at favorable times.

Environmental forecasting is vital to strategic planning; it considers the ways in which the company expects to expand and grow, and is the essential glue that holds the units of the company together, assuring a common purpose and direction. It also points out the need for new facilities,

Research planning based on technoeconomic forecasting is of key importance to any company likely to be affected by technological change—and this probably means most companies. It sets the direction of research activity, warns of the dangers of technological obsolescence, and points out new opportunities for profitable future growth.

Forecasts are becoming more and more important, because as industry becomes larger and more complicated, management finds it necessary to make larger commitments of capital for longer time periods. To insure success, management needs increasing amounts of information that shed light on the future.

Since business in the United States operates under laws intended to guarantee full and free competition, monopolies or cartels cannot be used to control the future environment.

Rather, management must guess at how to operate best in an uncertain future over which it has only limited control. Moreover, as businesses grow in scope and size, becoming more diversified in product line and geography, they face not only domestic but also global problems. Thus the uncertainties become more numerous and more complex.

Above all, forecasts are necessary to give corporate management an "image" of the company that it guides. Companies are often what they want themselves to be. An open-minded, optimistic vision of the future can lead to growth and profit; a narrow, pessimistic view can lead to stagnation or worse, as in the case of Sewell Avery and Montgomery Ward. But the main point to remember is that a forecast should have an objective. A forecast done merely to satisfy curiosity is of no value. A man who turns out forecasts not directly related to company problems can predict a hazardous future for his company.

The Scope of Forecasting

How far into the future should we look? As a rough rule of thumb, it might be expected that about two-thirds of the time a 5-year forecast will be within plus or minus 10 percent of the actual result; a 10-year forecast, plus or minus 20 percent; and a 25- to 35-year forecast, plus or minus as much as 50 percent. It would seem, therefore, that quantitative forecasts in great detail beyond 5 years are probably neither necessary nor useful.

On the other hand, certain types of forecasts are not useful unless they are made for more than 5 years ahead—or for as much as 35 years ahead—for example, in cases involving the accumulation of mineral resources. Most mining companies need long-term ore reserves to justify an operation, and they must also have some idea of future demands and trends.

The chronological scope of a forecast should be governed by its purpose and by the company's needs. A commodity trader is interested in the next few days or, at most, the next few months. Another company may find that, while five years are long enough to build a new plant and get it operating, or to enter a new market, a five-year forecast will not tell management all that it has to know, especially when it is dealing with the impact of major technological developments. And the company that wants to plant Douglas fir trees must guess at the next *hundred* years; it takes about that long to get a Douglas fir to pulping size. It is true that Keynes said, "In the long run we are all dead," but his statement referred to forecasters, not to their corporations. Corporations do not have to die.

The Forecaster

Who should forecast? Forecasting is difficult enough to warrant everybody's contribution—from the professional economist to the salesman who is on the front line of his company's business in daily contact with its customers. Forecasts should represent a coordinated rational synthesis of all kinds of experience and knowledge. The advantages of such a synthesis are that it brings into play specialized knowledge of all types and that it prevents dominance by one viewpoint or opinion. While forecasting is not scientific, it must rely on a fusion of skill and scientific methodology. The coordinator and synthesizer of the forecast must be a person who can understand and use scientific methodology; that is, a person who can make use of organized knowledge applied to an understanding of cause-and-effect relationships. Only in this way can he develop forecasts that are good enough to be useful.

What makes a good forecast? The determining factor is not the quality of the method, but the quality of the forecaster—primarily his flexibility and judgment. There may be better and worse methods of forecasting, but even the best technical method is not better than the judgment of the forecaster. Thus the difference is not between good and bad methods but between good and bad forecasters.

Who should not forecast? First, anyone who believes that the future is only a straight-line extrapolation of the past. We do not need a forecaster for this; all we need is a piece of graph paper, a pencil, and a ruler.

In studying the past in order to understand the future, we have to remember that to some extent past trends will continue, while to some extent structural changes will occur that will change the trends by

1. Changing the quantitative relationship of what we are trying to forecast to the influencing factor.
2. Introducing new influencing factors.
3. Bringing to the foreground influencing factors that were only of minor importance in the past.
4. Causing past factors of importance to become unimportant factors in the future.

Let us take an analogous case: A man meets a beautiful and intelligent girl, and decides to marry her, but then he finds out that she has been divorced three times. What are his chances for a lasting marriage with her? On the face of it, the record says little chance. But in all fairness, shouldn't he look beyond the numbers to see the basic reasons for the record? Have there been any changes in the girl? In the circumstances in which she lives? Are the causes of her divorces likely to repeat themselves in this fourth marriage?

A quote is appropriate here: "It is never possible to step twice into the same river." This was stated by Heraclitus, a Greek philosopher who lived about 500 B.C. He believed that the only reality is change, and that permanence is an illusion.

Who else should not forecast? The man who substitutes arithmetic for sense. Again a quote, this time from A. N. Whitehead, the British philosopher and mathematician: "There is no more common error than to assume that, because prolonged and accurate calculations have been made, the applicability of the result to some fact of nature is absolutely certain."

Who else should not forecast? The man who thinks he has the only magic formula. Probably the ultimate in forecasting is reached in trying to forecast stock prices. Stock prices fluctuate very sensitively in response to events both real and imagined. Is there a magic formula, or does main reliance have to be placed on economic knowledge, experience, and judgment? Anyone who has played the stock market knows the answer to that one. And if someone tells about his magic formula, remember the question you may have seen: "If you're so smart, why aren't you rich?" Also remember this:

A past article in *Forbes* magazine (October 1, 1965, p. 12) compared the performance of four groups of stocks with the Dow-Jones average. The groups were:

1. Stocks bought by small investors—the top 25 favorites of participants in the Monthly Investment Plan sponsored by the New York Stock Exchange.
2. The 25 favorite stocks of odd-lot purchasers.
3. The 25 favorite stocks of the Institutional Investors

Mutual Fund, which is the fund of New York State savings banks.

4. The 25 favorite stocks of financial institutions, such as insurance companies, investment companies, and common trust funds (as compiled by *Data Digest*).

In performance, measured since the start of 1961, the stock selectors ranked as follows, from best to worst, in their correlations with the Dow-Jones average:

1. Monthly Investment Plan participants.
2. Institutional investors.
3. Savings banks mutual funds—of course, they were closely governed by legal requirements.
4. Odd-lotters—were worst; actually lost money.

Unselling the Forecast

How does a forecaster sell his forecast to your management? Today we can assume that your management wants forecasts. The forecaster may not have to do too much to sell them, but he can easily unsell them. Here is a sure guide to the forecaster on unselling his forecast:

1. Complicate it with a lot of mathematical and statistical formulas and derivations, but also make some simple mistake in arithmetic, especially in addition or subtraction.
2. Don't let anyone else participate in making *your* forecast. You want it to be *yours* alone—why share credit? Stick to only one method and your own

thoughts. Don't let others confuse you with facts or with different results obtained by different methods.

3. Let the computer do the forecast. That way you won't need any ideas of your own. Just throw in the series you want to forecast, and keep throwing in possibly related series until you get a correlation equation with a high correlation coefficient. With a lot of variables it will look good, even if it doesn't work. Since you contribute nothing, you can at least claim that your forecast will be objective. This method is commonly called GIGO—garbage in, garbage out.

4. Dream up forecasting methods that do not rely on cause-and-effect relationships; involve hard-to-get, inaccurate data; and are expensive in time, manpower, and money.

5. Get the wrong results, but explain how you were really right. Show that you might have been way off, but were actually within the acceptable limits of statistical tests of significance.

6. Make every forecast final. Don't ever review it in the light of new data.

The Selection of Applicable Methods

Methods available for analysis and forecasting of product demand range all the way from pure hunches to pure mathematics. "Hunches" or intuitive judgments are arrived at through personal observations of the market, its characteristics, and its reactions. The influence of changing supply-and-demand conditions is observed. The observer sees the facts, but he usually does not consciously attempt to discover or use exact quantitative relationships to interpret them, even though he may be cognizant of these relationships and be able to derive valuable clues from them. The experienced observer can make hunches work in the same way that a driver can drive a car without knowing exactly how the car works. But the "huncher" must have experience, intuition, know-how, and time for observation and reflection. Unfortunately, he usually cannot explain his methods to others in terms of methodology or principles. Learning must be by trial and error.

Pure mathematical forecasting, if carried out in a mechanical fashion, is not a substitute for common sense and thought. The analyst and forecaster cannot be content to derive a correlation equation from statistical data based on past relationships and hope to forecast by merely inserting estimated values into the formula. The desirable approach is between these points, relying on a combination of sound personal judgment and the analysis of historical data.

Practical considerations in selecting a forecasting method should also be considered. One objection raised to the use of advanced statistical techniques such as multiple correlation is that they may be difficult to explain to executives who are not familiar with statistical concepts and procedures. The traditional collection of forecasts from salesmen and executives is of great value in combination with statistical techniques for both comparison and psychological purposes. Those who use a forecast will find it more acceptable if they have played a role in developing it. Certainly, the experience of salesmen and executives should not be ignored, and if they disagree with some of the results of forecasts made by strictly statistical methods, their opinions should be carefully examined and reconciled.

Obviously, the methods used to analyze and forecast the demand for (let us say) chemical commodities will be influenced by the problem at hand, the time and facilities available to the analyst, the knowledge and skill of the analyst, and the importance of the results. However, some general ground rules for good forecasting and analytical procedure can be set forth:

1. The analyst should know his field. Statistical analysis of data is only a tool. The researcher must have an adequate knowledge of the facts of his field, both technical and otherwise. A good forecast involves knowledge of trade channels, historical trends, end-use patterns, market shares, geographical factors, correlation with indicators, trade expectations, and political, psychological, and other technical and economic factors. Price forecasting especially requires a great background of knowledge. There will also be factors unique to each situation. Much of the trouble in forecasting is caused by unanticipated, noneconomic factors such as wars and strikes. The forecaster may not make such assumptions, but he should be prepared to judge the consequences of such events and their possible effects on his forecasts.

2. All forecasts are based on assumptions. The forecaster should know and be prepared to state his assumptions. These assumptions should cover both external and internal factors. External factors are those over which his company has no control: the state of the economy, competition, and so on. Internal factors are the result of policies set by the company in relation to such matters as inventories, product line, and quality. The forecaster must know his product, his industry, and his company.

3. The objective of the forecast must be clearly stated in terms of the question or questions to be answered. The mere collection of statistics and their analysis are of no use unless they are done with a purpose in mind.

4. Having his data on hand, the forecaster should de-

velop a hypothesis or tentative solution. This hypothesis should arise out of the theoretical and practical training of the analyst, literature searching, interviews, pilot studies, and all other means at his disposal of gathering pertinent facts. The analyst should study demand-controlling factors in order to determine the nature of their influence and their other characteristics. His selection of demand-controlling factors should be governed by the ease of forecasting such factors. Diagrammatic representations of the influence of controlling factors on commodity demand may be useful at this point.

5. Data pertinent to the hypothesis should be gathered, refined, and carefully checked. A well-defined and complete hypothesis expedites the gathering of pertinent numerical data completely and economically.

6. If possible, apparent relationships between commodity demand and influencing factors should be simply tested by graphic analysis. The graphic scatter chart is an essential prelude to mathematical manipulation. Actually, a graph contains more information than an equation; an equation is only a shorthand notation of the data. The scatter diagram, on the other hand, simultaneously shows both the individuality of each point and the general trend of all the points, which the equation cannot do. Mathematical equations do, however, emphasize the main movements. The value of the graph as a screening device cannot be overemphasized.

7. A simple hypothesis is both useful and practical. It should explain most of the changes in commodity demand, but it cannot explain all the data. It is very important for the analyst to discover how the small number of data that do not fit his hypothesis can be accounted for. Did extraordinary events not likely to recur affect commodity demand in a few of the years? Did normally minor controlling fac-

tors become of major importance in a few of the years? There is much to be learned by careful study of these "residuals," much that can be applied to future forecasts. In every forecast, the forecaster should consider not only the effects of the main controlling factors covered by his simple hypothesis but also all other possibilities.

8. No forecast should be accepted as final. All forecasts should be constantly reviewed in the light of the latest data. Each new datum contributes to the hypothesis and demonstrates the reliability or unreliability of the hypothesis used.

It is apparent from the evidence at hand that forecasting cannot be called an exact science. Certainly, the successful analyst must use every technique at hand to aid him in his work. The analyst has a special interest in the correlation method, because in many cases it is a shortcut numerical procedure. In addition, it is usually less expensive and less time consuming than some of the more elaborate procedures that require the gathering of larger amounts of data, such as the detailed end-use analysis approach, or the use of field surveys.

There is every indication that the use of regression equations to test historical, hypothetical relationships of commodity demand to associated variables is a valuable procedure if such equations are not used in an overly mechanical fashion. The analyst using the correlation procedure must be skillful in extrapolating these relationships into the future, and must modify their use by application of his own good judgment. In addition, he should by no means restrict himself to any one technique, but should use all possible data and techniques as supplementary aids.

The correlation procedure also has some very important limitations, even in cases where sufficient data for its use are available. It would appear to be most applicable to forecast for not less than one or more than five years ahead. For less than one year, survey methods may be of greatest value. For five years or more, the great number of required assumptions result in what might better be called a projection than a forecast. Probably only "crude projections" can be made for five or more years ahead by *any* method.

For three to four years ahead, even with independent variables forecast to within 5 to 10 percent of actual, forecasts derived without modification by mere substitution in a regression equation will probably be in error by more than 10 percent two-thirds of the time, and by more than 20 percent one-third of the time. It should be noted, however, that this range of accuracy applies to forecasts pinpointed for a given year. When year-to-year figures vary substantially, better results can probably be obtained if future forecasts are made for the average of a two- or three-year period. This type of forecast is often adequate for many purposes.

All methodology available for the analysis and forecasting of commodity demand, in order to be useful, should be based on the use of organized knowledge. The analyst should relate commodity demand to the factors that influence it, and attempt to extrapolate these influencing factors into the future. But in addition to studying the principal influencing variables and their effects, he should be careful to study the cases in which historical relationships may break down. There is no reason for historical economic relationships to continue indefinitely into the future. Nor is there any reason for the factors that influence industrial commodity demand to continue to act as they have in the past. Moreover, the analyst must always be on guard for new influencing variables.

Correlation analysis. Correlation analysis is one useful

method of evaluating historical data when such data are available. The newer techniques such as model-building and input-output analysis, despite recent interest in them, have not shown any significant advantage over correlation analysis, and in practice present many difficulties both in mathematical computation and in collection and integration of data. But correlation equations take into account only the principal influencing variables, and considerable skill is required on the part of the analyst to account for the effect of other influencing factors through the use of other techniques.

In actual forecasts, correlation analysis and detailed end-use analysis of industrial commodity demand appear to be very useful methods, often superior to expert opinion. On the other hand, the opinions of experts and executives should be carefully studied and taken into account. In many cases surveys are the only way of obtaining valuable data, especially where it is necessary to ascertain future intentions. But even the most skilled analyst cannot afford to neglect any of the tools or data available to him, and must constantly review his forecast if he is to achieve any degree of success.

Forecasting will probably never be an exact science, and precise results are not to be expected. The results will vary with the time period over which the forecast is made, the difficulty of the problem at hand, and the skill of the analyst. An intimate knowledge of the field under study is of utmost importance in solving the commodity demand problem. Statistical analysis of the data is only a test of the solution; actual use in forecasting is the real test of the value of the analysis.

Criteria for selecting methods. In selecting a method or methods on which to base his forecast, the analyst should consider the following criteria:

1. The method should be a scientific one, that is, based on the use of knowledge to explore cause-and-effect relationships.
2. It should be able to determine and measure cause-and-effect relationships, even if inexactly.
3. It must lend itself easily to forecasting purposes.
4. It must be based on the use of *available* data.
5. It should be inexpensive in terms of time and manpower, in relation to the accuracy and value of the results obtained, and the manpower should not be too difficult to hire or train.
6. Finally, and most importantly, it should work empirically and give useful forecasts.

We have stated that most forecasting methods are based on a study of historical relationships, and that these historical relationships will not necessarily continue unchanged in the future. This fact must be faced in practical forecasting work. Economic stability cannot be counted on. Often, short-period relationships can be derived and used where long-term relationships lack stability. In some cases, it may be helpful to consider broader sectors of the economy.

A forecast should be used as only one element in making business decisions. No one can make very good forecasts under the best of conditions, and even an exact forecast would not guarantee success and profit. On the other hand, since risks are related to profits, good forecasting can increase management's potential to make profit by extending its capability and willingness to assume a measure of risk.

A forecast, to repeat, is not by itself a basis for action. Forecasting assesses the future environment and the possible interactions between a company and its environment.

A forecast is a basis on which management can construct a plan—a structure of goals, policies, programs, and procedures—a guide to effective action. Forecasting can be delegated. Management decisions cannot.

2

A Survey of
Product Demand Forecasting
Methods

Mᴜᴄʜ has been written about the various methods of forecasting product demand. Many of these methods can be used to forecast both general business conditions and the demand for specific products. Generally, the techniques may be classified as (1) nonnumerical methods, based on qualitative appraisals related to the judgment and experience of individuals, and (2) methods employing extensive numerical devices, statistics, and mathematics, culminating in the methods of econometrics. The types of nonnumerical methods actually used are

1. Executive consensus.
2. Sales managers' estimates.
3. Historical analogy.
4. Industry experts' composites.
5. Sampling of group opinions.
6. Simple ratio method.
7. Delphi method.

The numerical methods include

1. Correlation analysis.
2. Equation systems or models.
3. End-use analysis.
4. Input-output analysis.
5. Trend and cycle analysis.

Nonnumerical Methods

Nonnumerical methods avoid the use of large masses of historical data and their mathematical manipulation. Numerical data used for determining variables must be handled very carefully, since many of the data are subject to inaccuracy, change, and revision.

Executive consensus. This method is practiced extensively in businesses today. An outside organization may furnish data on trends and competition, but it is the executives of the particular company who ultimately develop the forecast. A conference is held so that each executive can state his views and the reasons for them, and the chairman of the group coordinates the various opinions in order to form some positive decision on policy.

Some of the advantages of this method are that it is simple and familiar in operation, and that the forecast can be made quickly. It does not require the preparation of elaborate statistics, and it may be the only possible method if adequate data are not available for other methods. Furthermore, it brings together a wide variety of specialized viewpoints: the views and judgments of all the key men who know the firm and its products, and who are responsible for profits and operations.

Some of the method's disadvantages, inherent in its basic subjectivity, are that it rests entirely on personal opinion, and may be largely guesswork; since no standard procedure is established, there is no real way of weighing and evaluating individual opinions. In addition, there is a great expenditure of executive time on work for which the executives may not be suited. The breakdown by products, time intervals, and markets may be very difficult for sales and operating personnel to make, and many top executives are frequently not aware of economic trends. Finally, the assumptions that are necessarily involved in all forecasts are not usually brought out formally in these conferences, so that the wrong and right assumptions cannot be traced.

Actually, the experience of executives should not be by-passed in any forecasting system. Moreover, executives using a forecast should feel that they have had some hand in its preparation. But care should be taken to provide executives with statistically prepared materials that will give them a realistic point of departure, a common basis for their views, and valid assumptions for their appraisal.

Sales managers' estimates. The method involving sales managers' estimates is the "grass roots" approach. The theory is that the sales managers are closer to the users of the product and have a better view of prospects than do the executives. Information is obtained from the sales managers by questionnaires or conferences. Each questionnaire must be carefully phrased, simple, and unambiguous, and must include information on all known policies and changes that the company expects to make. It must be uniform for all districts, containing enough material to check both for internal consistency and against known facts. It is important to choose the correct time of year in which to collect information; the best time may be the end of the year, when the entire year's experience is available for study.

The advantages of this method are that the responsibility for the forecast rests in the man who must meet the goals, and that the specialized knowledge of the men who are closest to the customers and the market is utilized. Because of this, the method instills confidence into the salesmen and sales executives, since the forecast is their own creation. Since the method generally involves a large number of contributors, even though details may be quite in error, errors in totals tend to be canceled out. No technical knowledge is required of the men who work with this method, and it is likely that the information that they need has already been broken down by product and territory. Unlike most other types of forecasts, this forecast is built from the bottom up.

The disadvantages of the method are that the sales manager, who is concerned with distribution, may be unaware of national developments and trends. Even if he does know local trends, he may not be able to translate them quantitatively into a forecast. Salesmen are generally poor estimators, and may be especially inaccurate in judging long-term trends. Optimistic or pessimistic according to current conditions, they are usually optimistic with rising sales and pessimistic with declining sales. The sales manager relies heavily on the current position of his sales and the feel of the market. Moreover, salesmen are torn between the desire to forecast low, in order to make their sales records look good by comparison, and the desire to forecast high, in order to impress the central office with their possibilities. Another disadvantage of this method is that it draws heavily on the time of the personnel who make the forecast. When this is considered, the cost appears high in comparison with other methods, and the method itself becomes slower and more cumbersome as the company expands.

The sales managers' estimate approach has long been a very popular method, and is still considered by many to be the most valuable one. On the other hand, one of the most significant developments in forecasting is the increasing use of statistics. Some companies now bypass the traditional salesmen's estimates entirely, with the feeling that good salesmen are optimistic and therefore cannot be very objective.

Historical analogy. Known in the field of stock price forecasting as "chart reading," this method involves the comparison of characteristics and trends in similar situations. It can be most readily used in analyzing new product sales or similar patterns of sales, but it has many pitfalls. The major one is that economic patterns are rarely the same at any two given points, and that there is no information available on turning points. Followers of this method will recognize the high degree of subjectivity that it involves; it is used only as a last resort, or along with other methods.

Industry experts' composite figures. In this method, the company periodically asks experts in individual fields to submit forecasts, which are then combined and weighted. The advantage of the method is that it combines opinions of experts in specific fields, and thus produces a forecast with details of various industries. It is used mainly by multiproduct companies with national distribution. The disadvantage is that there is no way of correlating the different parts, whereas a total forecast must be coordinated and interlocked. On the other hand, the method may be of great value in certain problems, such as a forecast of the Federal Reserve Board production index, which is a composite of several industries.

Sampling of group opinions. This method deals with future intentions, as in the case of the McGraw-Hill survey of plant expenditures or the Federal Reserve Board survey of consumer intentions. *Fortune* magazine and Dun and Bradstreet conduct similar surveys, which indicate qualitative rather than quantitative data. The problem lies both in weighting and in sampling. The method requires very expert sampling, and usually calls for the repetition of work at frequent intervals to check opinion trends. This method is good for new products, where other approaches may not be possible, since it can predict such variables as style shifts. Unfortunately, adequate sampling can be done only at a very high cost.

Ratio method. This is a frequently used device, a naive extrapolation of the previous year's trend. It assumes that the percent change in sales from the previous year to the current year will be the same for the current year to the coming year.

The Delphi method. The Delphi method is a new method developed in the past decade by RAND Corporation to forecast technology, and is especially useful in research planning. In this technique, experts are individually asked to state their views as to the timing and likelihood of new technology. The opinions are recirculated anonymously, so that each expert can view the varied opinions and modify his own if he desires to do so. This eventually results in a unified consensus that is of more value than the original raw results. Exhibit 1 illustrates a typical format for use in this method.

Exhibit 1

Typical Form for Use in Delphi Method

Survey of New Technology
1969

We are making a survey of new technological developments likely to affect our business. In line with this, as a first step, we would appreciate your listing those you consider important, with an indication of the time when they would take place, in the space below:

Name:

Organization:

Address:

Phone: Area Code   Number   Extension

Significant Developments in New Technology That May Affect Our Product Line, Present or Potential	*Period in Which This Development Is Most Likely to Happen* *(Check one)*				
	1968– 1970	*1971– 1975*	*1976– 1980*	*1981– 1985*	*1986– 1990*
1.					
2.					
3.					

Bayesian analysis. Judgment techniques can be very successful. The forecaster who uses judgment may be likened to the art expert who looks at a Picasso to judge whether it is fake or not. In his mind he has synthesized his past experience and knowledge and sees the picture as a whole. He may not be able to describe exactly what his thought processes are, but he can come up with a verdict. Probably a computer could do no better. Above all, judgment implies subjectivity, and judgment will be relative. As an economist once said, a "recession" is when the man next to you gets fired; a "depression" is when *you* get fired.

Numbers and statistics can be misused. There is the story of the statistician who was afraid of someone planting a bomb on a plane. Whenever he flew, he worried. The statistics showed that there had been bombs planted on one of every 10,000 flights. The statistician also estimated that if the probability of one bomb was 1 in 10,000, then the chances of two bombs on one flight would be only 1 in 100 million. He solved his problem by always carrying a bomb with him, thus reducing the chance of another bomb to an absurdly low number.

In recent years, numerical and judgment techniques have been married in a technique known as Bayesian Analysis. This is remotely derived from a theorem proposed by the Reverend Thomas Bayes, an eighteenth-century English clergyman who stated that it is legitimate to quantify our feelings about uncertainty in terms of subjectively assessed numerical probabilities, even for a unique decision, where historical data do not exist. In practice, this means that we can assign a probability to each forecast submitted by a salesman, and combine probabilities to assess numerically the likelihood of the combined forecast—all based on judgment.

Numerical Methods

Numerical methods tend to be more objective than nonnumerical ones, and generally cost no more, considering the amount of executive and salesman time consumed by nonnumerical methods. Numerical methods, if properly used, are reliable and rapid in estimating the "normal" trend, thus leaving more time to analyze the details of deviations from this norm. Simple graphical methods can be used when less accurate estimates are acceptable, and various other short cuts and extrapolations are possible when some direct data are not available. Furthermore, even when a specific product involves only a few people, its sales are generally linked with economic indicators and other demand factors that involve many people and agencies; the scope of data collection is thus broadened considerably, and the analyst has the benefit of collective analysis and judgment.

On the other hand, there is a danger, in depending solely on numerical methods, of abandoning individual and independent judgment, and of placing too heavy a reliance on the arbitrary nature of mathematics. This in turn leads to the chance of error through completely unforeseen or unpredictable variations from the norm—for example, political factors or other basic assumptions that are not within the scope of mathematics. Often, not enough care is taken to relate effect to cause. Or there may be difficulty in breaking down the complete analysis into details for individual products and territories.

Numerical methods generally demand the talents of specialists, because most of the methods are difficult to explain to salesmen, production men, and executives who lack a background in statistics. But these are the men who will have to follow the quotas derived from the methods, and it is essential that they have confidence both in the forecast and in the way it was developed.

Correlation analysis. The procedure of correlation analysis in forecasting involves measuring the relationship among certain factors or groups of factors that are thought to be related to the product demand. On the basis of these measurements and certain further assumptions, the future demand for the product is estimated. This method should be carefully distinguished from mere mathematical projection of time trends using original data and per capita data.

Although correlation analysis is designed to give quantitative results, qualitative indications will often be sufficient. For example, the only thing needed may be an indication of a cycle's change of direction. In this case, recently devised methods of forecasting turns in economic cycles by the frequency of changes in indicator series (classified as lead, lag, or current) may be adapted to indicate qualitative changes in product demand.

Work in the field of econometrics has indicated that conventional least-squares correlation methods are special cases of a broader method of describing the economy by systems of equations, that is, models. This by no means negates the simpler method; single equations give as good results for forecasting as do equation systems. However, in some cases the equation system may give the analyst a better insight into the demand forces—for example, where dependent and independent variables in the simple equation are actually mutually interdependent. This condition of mutual interdependence is not often found in cases concerned with manufactured products.

The correlation equation is a practical device whose value in forecasting can be determined only by its success in actual use. It is designed to make use only of the major demand factors that account for most of the variation in demand, the assumption being that the net result of the many other minor demand forces interact in a random way, so that the small, unaccounted-for residuals are randomly distributed. Often, however, such minor factors become so important that, unless they are modified, they can render the historical relationship valueless.

There is little point in discussing in detail the statistical regression technique used in correlation analysis, as it is well covered in many statistics textbooks. Even more important than the regression technique itself are the modifications that the forecaster must make in it to obtain a useful forecast. The regression technique has many limitations that make it a dangerous weapon in the hands of the unskilled. For one thing, the basic economic relationships must be understood before correlation equations can be established. The use of economic flow diagrams and models is a valuable aid in this regard.

Some analysts insist on trying to achieve perfect fit in their regression equations. Most experienced analysts, however, concentrate on explaining a substantial part of the variation, realizing that imperfection of fit is caused not only by partial or incorrect explanations of variation (such as the omission of variables) but also by errors in data and the intercorrelation of independent variables. Closeness of fit with the time period included in the analysis is not enough; the residuals from regression equations must be studied carefully. Unless they are small and random, they must be explainable in order for the equation to be useful. The analyst must ask himself the following questions:

1. Are the large residuals of the regression likely to occur in the future?

2. Will certain factors, which were negligible in the past, have an important influence in the future—such factors as regional consumption patterns, income distribution, and population age distributions?
3. Are the leads and lags represented in the equation likely to remain the same in the future?

These are only some of the problems involved in extrapolating regressions into the future in order to make a successful forecast.

Statistical tests of significance are based on probability theory, which does not strictly cover economic time series, because of the presence of serial correlation and interdependence of successive observations. However, statistical measures are rough guides. It may be said that regression equations of demonstrated value usually have high correlations, with r over 0.9.

Most forecasters do not rely solely on statistical tests of significance, but rely also on empirical testing of relationships in actual forecasts, and on the use of common sense in formulating relationships that reflect economic realities. Such experts as Fox and Yates have repeatedly pointed out the dangers of depending on statistical measurements to the exclusion of scientific logic and common sense. According to them, if there were no logical reason for expecting a systematic relationship between two sets of numbers, we would expect that, when one variable was graphed against the other variable, the observations would be so widely scattered that no systematic upward or downward drift or slope would appear. However, if the number of observations (logically unrelated) were small, we would not infrequently find that these graphs or scatter diagrams *looked* as though there were a definite regression relationship.

If each of two series contains only two observations, these four observations define two points through which only one straight line can be drawn, and it is quite likely that the slope of such a line will not be exactly zero. Sets of three or four logically unrelated observations will also quite frequently suggest (to the eye) a definite relationship. But as the number of observations in two unrelated series increases, the great majority of samples will show a wide scatter and no line will appear to be of much use for estimating value of one series from specified values of the other.

Many economic time series show strong trends; population has increased steadily, as have output per man-hour per man-year and prices of goods and services. If a scatter diagram is made showing paired observations of two time series that have no known logical relationship but each of which contains a strong trend, the scatter will suggest a high degree of relationship between the two variables. The average value of one will increase (or decrease) steadily as the other increases over time. In such cases, statistical tests will suggest that the relationship can hardly be due to chance. If there is no *logical* basis for expecting a permanently close association between two series, the relationship has no practical usefulness or safe interpretation, since *any two linear trends will be perfectly correlated.*

A statistician once wrote: "With statistics, the unscrupulous deceive the unwary and the innocent deceive themselves." This statement is applicable to the interpretation of regression relationships based on time series. The temptation to build causal explanations around the trend elements in possibly unrelated time series can be very strong.

Simple regressions involve only two variables. However, most problems of importance in economic theory and in real economic behavior involve more than two simultaneously changing variables, and some involve several distinct equations operating simultaneously or with time lags. Hence it is particularly important that we see the mechanics and arithmetic of simple regression analysis against a realistic economic background.

The adoption of more powerful methods of mathematical statistics is no panacea. If econometric results are more useful today than in the past, it is only partially because of particular methods of estimation; much more significantly, it is because of research—painstaking research of a more pedestrian nature. The building of reality into formulations of economic relationships and the refinement of basic data collection have contributed much more to the improvement of empirical econometric results than have more elaborate methods of statistical inference. Through better knowledge of the functioning of economic institutions, through the use of new measurements on variables, and through the use of more accurate data, we can look forward to great improvements in the precision of our econometric judgments, improvement of as much as 50 percent. In contrast, we should expect marginal improvements of only 5 or 10 percent through the use of more powerful methods of statistical inference. All routes to improvement must be followed, since any gains are precious, no matter how small, and yet different contributions should be kept in proper perspective.

Analysts often tend to overemphasize statistical tests of significance. Unfortunately, the emphasis on these tests and the consideration of the isolated results of each experiment have often meant that scientific workers regard the execution of a test of significance as the ultimate objective. Results are significant or not, and that is the end of it.

The tendency to base the interpretation of data entirely on the results of significance tests has its dangers. Many workers apply significance tests excessively, sometimes at the expense of sound judgment and a careful overall assessment of the work. A sound interpretation will take into account, not only such individual tests as are made, but also prior knowledge and experience and the general consistency of the demonstrated effects. Research workers, therefore, have to accustom themselves to the fact that in many branches of economic research the really critical study is rare, and that it is frequently necessary to combine the results of numbers of studies dealing with the same issue in order to form a satisfactory picture of the true situation.

Equation systems or models. Much attention has recently been given to the use of systems of equations rather than single equations in forecasting both the economy and the demand for specific commodities. However, as we have pointed out, although models may aid in analysis, single equations are sufficient for forecasting. Outside of agricultural commodity demand forecasting, little practical use has been made of equation systems in product forecasting.

While the equation-system approach appears promising, its principal handicaps are inadequate mathematical models and statistical methods based on assumptions that are not strictly true. The construction of a model is very complicated, although most model building shown in literature on the subject suggests many possibilities but is highly simplified. The usefulness of this method as an aid and supplement to single equations in forecasting manufactured product demand is generally undemonstrated.

End-use analysis. The previous methods discussed might be termed macromethods in that they deal with aggregates. In any aggregative treatment of economic variables, the fact that the microstructure is not known is a handicap. On the other hand, it is assumed that the product analyst will be well aware of both the macro- and microstructure of the economic sector with which he is dealing, and will use all pertinent factors in constructing his hypotheses and interpreting his results. The aggregate method may be looked upon as a shortcut method of treating data that is based on the assumption that microdata are subject to the laws of probability and can be treated in the aggregate.

End-use analysis is a method involving the breaking down of a commodity into its end-use pattern, studying each of these small sectors individually by means of all known forecasting techniques, and then recombining these elements into the aggregate. The method has been very popular in the petroleum industry, and it may be the only method in forecasting new-product demand, where little or no data are available.

Input-output analysis. The method of input-output analysis developed by Leontief 25 years ago may be termed a combination of the simultaneous equation model and end-use analysis into a grand total system that attempts to include the economic interdependence of the national economy in one package. As Leontief pointed out in formulating his system, the forecaster is confronted with three rather different sets of questions:

1. What is the general state of the nation's business? (This level of analysis is usually in terms of aggregate national income and employment, and uses general indices of business activities.)
2. What is the outlook for a single industry, or for one specific product or type of product?
3. What are the sales prospects of a particular firm?

The answer to a question asked on a lower level of analysis depends partially on the answers given on the higher level, and partially on additional factors and considerations peculiar to that particular lower level. It is natural, says Leontief, to tie the analysis of a single industry's outlook to the forecast of the general level of economic activity. But to do it properly, one must know a lot about the specific problems of the industry in question. It is equally sensible to approach the estimate of future sales of a specific product of a specific company through a general study of factors determining the share of this particular company in the aggregate demand for the particular product; but this cannot be done without a thorough knowledge of the sales conditions for that particular product and company. The relationships hold true among all levels: An industry is a group of firms, and a nation is a group of industries and consumers.

Leontief holds that while the traditionally tried and proven method of estimating future demand of the product of an industry uses correlation of time series, such a system may break down suddenly, especially in periods of rapid change or in periods of stable and steady growth with little or no change, as in prewar and postwar periods; the formal, mechanical nature of the correlation makes it difficult to obtain a detailed analysis of the actual material relationships underlying the statistical correlation. Therefore, he maintains, structural market analysis or input-output analysis must support, supplement, or even replace correlation analysis.

In structural market analysis, the first question is: Who buys the product and how much does each buyer buy? Ultimately, this type of analysis must lead to simultaneous consideration of all industries and customers. A statistical description of this static system was conceived by Leontief to show diagrammatically the situation in any one year. An input-output chart is arranged in checkerboard fashion, with all producing sectors on the vertical axis and all consuming industries on the horizontal axis. Each figure in this table is a record of transfer of money from a buyer to a seller. The sum of the horizontal columns is the total gross output of an industry, or its total sales to all other industries and consumers. The sum of the vertical columns is the total gross outlay of each industry obtained by totalling its purchases from all other industries and suppliers. In other words, the table is a double-entry bookkeeping record of the purchases and sales of all sectors of the economy.

It immediately comes to mind that a demand for product A will mean a demand for the materials B and C required to make product A; B and C are products of some other industry, and this process is repeated *ad infinitum.* With modern, high-speed calculators, it is possible to sum up, not only the direct effect of an increase in the demand for product A on the demand for the primary materials B and C, but also the indirect effect throughout the economy by tracing the increased demand for the materials to make B and C, and the materials to make those materials, and so on *ad infinitum,* or at least to the practical point where the effects are negligible.

The principal defect of the input-output method is that it requires a great amount of facts and calculations, as compared with correlation methods. Unfortunately, little has been done to provide enough data to make the method useful for detailed forecasting. Furthermore, because of the complexity of the method, input-output tables are several years old by the time they become available.

Up to now, the work in this method has been largely on static models. The dynamic aspects of the method appear to present many problems with respect to practical application and theory. Dynamic relationships would probably have to be worked out by setting up correlation equations for each of the hundreds of sectors of the input-output table to show how the sector interrelationships vary as time passes. This is theoretically possible, but the data and computations required present an immense task. Moreover, dynamic relations would have to reflect not only the product flow but also the changes over time in the stock and in the nature of producing resources.

Trend and cycle analysis. The basic fault of fitting time trend lines and cycles is that time series fitted to time trends require unreasonable assumptions of the stability of long-run economic forces, particularly the assumption that the series move in a regular fashion with the passage of time.

Time series analysis of this type is consistent only with static equilibrium economics, and its vogue has declined in recent years. The dynamics of economic relationships over time are usually too variable to permit projections by any statistical methods that do not assist the *understanding* of past relationships. The use of time trends alone indicates wholehearted acceptance of the past as indicating, without qualification, the patterns of the future—with time as the only factor that influences change in commodity demand. There is no attempt to search out and measure the other forces in the economy that are associated with changes in commodity demand. In regression analysis, while assumptions are also made that past relationships continue into the future, the hypothethical relationships are at least supposed to be among many variables arising from a common causal system. Trained analysts use the time-trend method with extreme reluctance. Because the standard error is very large in a forecast from a curve of this type, the analyst is not justified in extrapolating the trend very far into the future.

But some analysts favor the time trend, claiming that the trend projection is the most direct statistical method available. The correlation method, they say, has some advantages but is more laborious, and in practice is generally less flexible, because mathematical relationships imply a continuation in the future of linear or curvilinear relationships that have existed in the past. The correlation method is probably the best one to use for a forecast that is to be made for only a year or two in the future, particularly if the value of one or more of the dependent variables can be estimated with reasonable accuracy. However, for forecasts over a longer period, the additional labor involved may not seem to justify its use.

Any method of forecasting is subject to a wide margin of error, and results should be accepted with considerable skepticism. A great number of assumptions have to be made to support the simple trend method when it is applied to the analysis of product demand:

1. Past trends will continue.
2. Extraneous factors and disturbing elements will not be present.
3. Population will continue to grow at a steady rate.
4. Consumers' tastes for the products considered will not change radically because of the introduction of substitute products.
5. Cheaper raw materials will not be discovered.
6. Moderately high levels of employment and income will be maintained.
7. Normal trade relations with other countries will be maintained.

8. There will be no serious disturbances of the economy by war or serious depression.

If all these assumptions are fulfilled, there is little or no point in using techniques more complicated than simple trend analysis. On the other hand, regression equations allow for change in each of these factors, according to the judgment of the analyst, thus giving relationships of greater flexibility than those in which time is the only factor. It would seem that the use of time alone as a factor in an economic relationship increases dependence on the assumptions implicit in the relationship. In effect, the analyst who uses time trends exclusively pays for their extreme simplicity with a loss of flexibility.

Trend projections are made mostly by semilogarithmic curves. Four well-known growth curves are

1. Gompertz.
2. Pearl-Reed or logistic.
3. Modified exponential.
4. Logarithmic parabola.

The Gompertz curve is the most often used for forecasting product demand. The Gompertz and Pearl-Reed curves are typically S-shaped and can be held to represent three phases of growth:

- Initial introduction.
- Rapid growth.
- Approach to maturity.

Both curves were borrowed from the biological sciences, and show continuously declining percentage rates of growth. The Gompertz curve is favored, because it shows a more gradual approach to maturity than the Pearl-Reed.

Difficulty often arises when the trend method is used to pinpoint forecasts for a specific period. On the other hand, under certain conditions the method may be the only applicable one. Relationships derived from the 1929–1940 period, in which there was a varied business cycle, may not hold for the 1946–1969 period of a steadily growing economy without significant cyclic movements. In this more recent period, application of a steady trend relationship may be the only practical forecasting method for many products.

Another difficulty in this method is the large number of years of data required to demonstrate the existence of a growth curve. Growth curves may require data of as many as 50 years to exhibit curvature, since use of only 20 to 30 years of data may show up as a straight line on semilogarithmic paper. Often, however, 18 to 24 years of data may suffice.

The Gompertz curve is of such a nature as to yield an ultimate constant value or asymptote. In many of these curves derived for products, the asymptotic or limiting values are absurdly low.

Care must also be taken not to start the data with years at the bottom of the business cycle, since use of such starting points would only yield a J-shaped rather than an S-shaped curve. On the other hand, starting with a high point in the cycle, such as 1929, may easily give an S-shaped curve that is not a true growth curve. Not all series give growth curves. For example, U.S. chemical sales from 1904 to 1969 will give only a straight-line trend on semilogarithmic paper, without significant indication of maturity.

One of the various difficulties in the conventional micro-end-use analysis approach is not foreseeing new end-uses over periods of two to three years, especially where markets are diffuse. The study of the change in product demand over time is one way of overcoming this defect; another lies in the correlation method, which links product demand to various associated economic factors.

3

Simple Numerical Techniques

Basically, there are four steps in forecasting:

1. Analyze the demand—the relationship of the commodity to the variables that affect it, and the measurement of this relationship.
2. Obtain a forecast of the independent variables.
3. Prepare a forecast for the commodity, using the forecast of the independent variables and adjusting for other factors not specifically included in the relationships derived from the demand analysis.
4. Demonstrate the value of the method through actual use. The final test of any method is, of course, its demonstrated practical usefulness.

This is the age of the computer. But while it takes only miniseconds for the computer to solve problems, much more time is consumed in feeding in data, getting a program, and waiting for computer time. Moreover, very few people have a computer at their fingertips. But there are some simpler tools: a pencil, a pad of writing paper, and a piece of graph paper—perhaps a slide rule, or an adding machine, or a small desk or portable calculator. When the boss calls at nine and wants an answer at five or over a weekend, and a sales projection has to be made, perhaps for some unfamiliar commodity or company, these tools plus a standard set of economic forecasts available from many sources should suffice for a quick answer. Numerical methods that lend themselves to pencil-pad and/or graph paper analysis are trend and cycle analysis, correlation, end-use analysis, and simple ratio analysis.

Trend and Cycle Analysis

As we have pointed out, the use of simply extrapolated time trends is easy, but has too many limitations in practice. Since the statistical methods involved can be found in any standard business statistics text, let us summarize them quickly:

If the future is thought of only as the continuation of the past, the "time series" is said to have a secular trend. When the time series is plotted on graph paper it will be found that a straight line can often be drawn through the clusters of points. (See Exhibit 2.) This line represents the correlation equation:

$$\text{Shipments} = a(\text{year}) + b.$$

In this equation, as in all others given for these charts,

$$a = \text{slope of line, that is } \frac{\text{change on x-axis}}{\text{change on y-axis}}$$

$b =$ point at which line, extended, crosses y-axis.

Exhibit 2

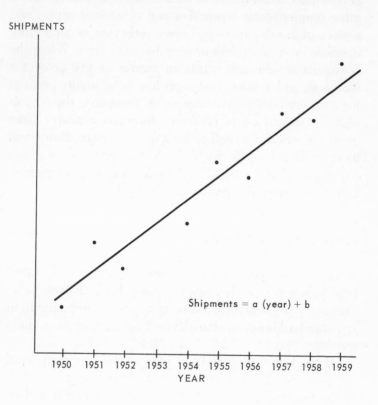

Shipments = a (year) + b

On the other hand, if the series is growing at a constant rate, say 10 percent per year, the line will be curved. (See Exhibit 3.) On semilog paper, where shipments are plotted on a log scale and time on an arithmetic scale, this type of series will be a straight line. The formula used in such charts is the same as that used to derive compound interest:

$$\text{Final sum} = \text{initial sum} (\text{interest rate})^{\text{year}}.$$

50

Not all points will be on the trend line. If each point represents an annual value, the deviations may show a cycle of two or three years duration, as in Exhibit 4. If the points are monthly or quarterly values, the deviations may show a seasonal trend that repeats itself each year, as in Exhibit 5. The residue of "irregular" is the difference between the actual values and the calculated values obtained from the secular trend, cycle, and seasonal variations.

Exhibit 3

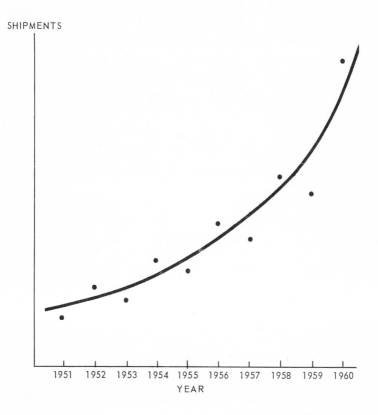

SHIPMENTS

1951 1952 1953 1954 1955 1956 1957 1958 1959 1960

YEAR

Exhibit 4

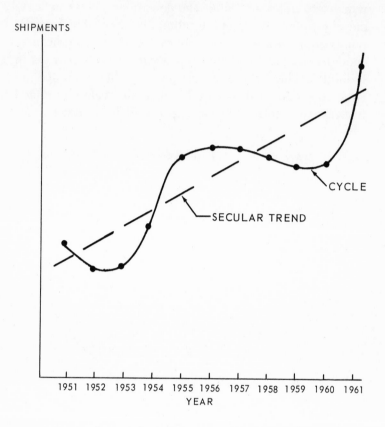

SHIPMENTS

CYCLE

SECULAR TREND

1951 1952 1953 1954 1955 1956 1957 1958 1959 1960 1961

YEAR

In actuality, time trends are a special case of correlation in which whatever is being forecast is correlated only to time. More benefit may be derived from using a correlation to an economic indicator.

Simple Correlation to Economic Indicators

Many people forecast the movement of such major economic indicators as the gross national product (GNP) and its components and the Federal Reserve Board (FRB) production index and its components. Few people forecast the demand for a specific industrial commodity, but we can make such a forecast by relating the commodity demand to an economic indicator. The quickest way to show this relationship is by a graph.

Exhibit 6 illustrates the relationship between industrial commodity shipments and the GNP, where the correlation equation is:

Industrial commodity shipments = a(GNP) + b.

Exhibit 5

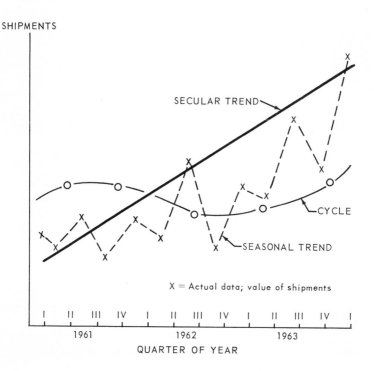

SHIPMENTS

SECULAR TREND

CYCLE

SEASONAL TREND

X = Actual data; value of shipments

| I | II | III | IV | I | II | III | IV | I | II | III | IV | I |

1961   1962   1963

QUARTER OF YEAR

Exhibit 6

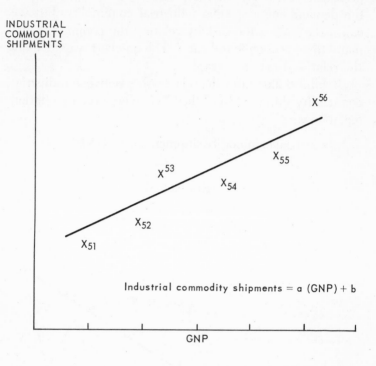

The years are noted next to their data points to aid in the analysis. Every mathematical derivation, whether by computer or by pencil, should be preceded by graphing.

For example: Packings are layers of material put between surfaces of a joint, mainly for the purpose of sealing moving parts. We might be hard pressed to find anyone interested in forecasting packings as such, but since packings go into a wide variety of products, a quick way to make a forecast is by relating packing shipments to an economic indicator that has been related to packing shipments in the past. (See Exhibit 7.) Thus a forecast of the

Exhibit 7

Relationship of Packings to FRB Index

Year*	Production Index (1957–59 = 100)	U.S. Shipments of Packings		
		$ Millions		Actual as Percent of Calculated
		Actual	Calculated**	
1947	66	$ 52	$ 52	100%
1954	86	65	74	114
1958	93	81	82	99
1963	125	117	117	100

* Data are available only for major census years.
** Calculated from relationship: U.S. shipments of packings = 1.11 (FRB production index) —21.

FRB production index—obtainable from many companies or other sources—can enable us to forecast packings.

Why the large error in 1954? We should study all such large errors carefully, because they may indicate that we have selected a poor or invalid relationship. In this case, 1954 is the first full year after the Korean War, and this may account for a below-normal demand. On the other hand, investigation might show data errors.

Here is another example: Shipments of printing ink are closely related to activity in the printing industry as measured by the Federal Reserve Board index for printing production. (See Exhibit 8.) Not many people forecast the FRB printing index, but the FRB printing index can be forecast from the GNP in constant dollars. (See Exhibit 9.)

The conventional way of calculating the mathematical relationships involves least-squares correlation, a tedious task without a computer. The computation might take two

Exhibit 8

Relationship of Printing Ink to FRB Printing Index

Year	FRB Printing Index (1957–59 = 100)	Shipments of Printing Ink Industry		Shipments, Actual as Percent of Calculated**
		($ Million)	Calculated* ($ Million)	
1947	70	$116	$125	93%
1948	73	N.A.	135	—
1949	75	130	142	92
1950	79	144	155	93
1951	80	161	158	102
1952	80	177	158	112
1953	84	179	171	105
1954	87	184	181	102
1955	93	199	201	99
1956	97	217	214	102
1957	99	229	221	104
1958	97	228	214	107
1959	104	240	237	101
1960	110	245	257	95
1961	112	252	264	95
1962	115	266	274	97
1963	116	268	277	97
1964	123	300	300	100

* Printing ink ($ millions) = 3.30 (FRB printing index) −106.
** Average error = 4%.
N.A. Not available.

or three hours with a desk calculator when a small number of years and one economic factor are involved—or as much as seven to eight hours when multiple correlations with two economic independent variables are involved.

To calculate these numerical relationships quickly, we

Exhibit 9

Relationship of FRB Printing Index to GNP in Constant Dollars

Year	GNP ($ Billions, 1958)	FRB Printing Index (1957–59 = 100)		Index, Actual as Percent of Calculated**
		Actual	Calculated*	
1947	$310	70	69	101%
1948	324	73	72	101
1949	324	75	72	104
1950	355	79	78	101
1951	383	80	84	95
1952	395	80	87	92
1953	413	84	90	93
1954	407	87	89	98
1955	438	93	96	97
1956	446	97	97	100
1957	453	99	99	100
1958	447	97	98	99
1959	476	104	104	100
1960	488	110	106	104
1961	497	112	108	104
1962	530	115	115	100
1963	550	116	119	97
1964	578	123	125	98
1965	609	130	131	99

* FRB printing index (1957–59=100) = .207 (GNP, $ billions, 58 $) + 5. Korean War years (1951–53) were omitted in calculation of relationship.
** Average error = 2%.

Exhibit 10

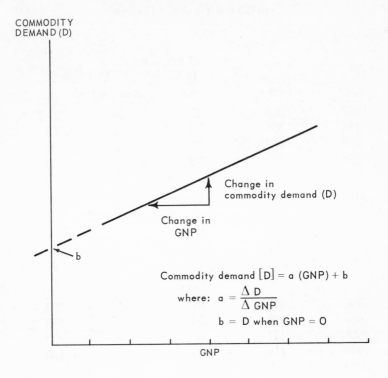

might begin with a graph like the one in Exhibit 10. In the equation

Commodity demand = a(GNP) + b,

the constant *b* is the point on the correlation line, drawn on the graph by judgment, where the GNP equals zero. The constant *a* is the slope of the line, that is, the value obtained by dividing any given change in commodity demand along the correlation line by the corresponding change in GNP.

There is also a shortcut method of calculating these

Exhibit 11

Relationship of Total Chemical Industry
to Gross National Product

Year	Gross National Product ($ Billions)	Chemical Industry Shipments		Chemical Industry Shipments, Actual as Percent of Calculated**
		Actual ($ Billions)	Calculated* ($ Billions)	
1947	$231	$10.1	$ 8.9	113%
1948	258	10.5	10.6	99
1949	266	10.9	11.2	97
1950	285	13.1	12.4	106
1951	328	15.5	15.1	103
1952	346	15.6	16.3	96
1953	365	16.6	17.5	95
1954	365	17.5	17.5	100
1955	398	19.7	19.6	101
1956	419	21.3	21.0	101
1957	441	22.3	22.4	100
1958	447	23.1	22.8	101
1959	484	26.3	25.1	105
1960	504	26.5	26.4	100
1961	520	27.2	27.4	99
1962	560	29.3	30.0	98
1963	591	31.8	32.0	99
1964	632	34.3	34.6	99

* Shipments ($ billions) = .0641 (GNP, $ billions) −5.9.
** Average error = 3%.

lines mathematically, which gives results close to those obtained with the least-squares method, especially when the relationship is close. For example, let us look at the relationship between chemical industry sales and the gross national product, as shown in Exhibit 11. The shortcut

Exhibit 12

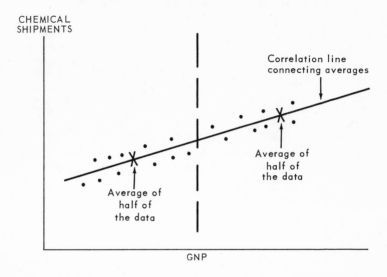

method involves dividing the data in half and then calculating the average of each half and the line that connects the two points, as in Exhibit 12.

The relationship of the total chemical industry shipments to the GNP, as shown in the table, was derived as follows: In the equation

$$\text{Chemical industry shipments} = a(\text{GNP}) + b,$$

we want to estimate a and b. The data are divided in two, and averages for each group are estimated:

	Average Value *($ Billions)*	
	9 Years *1947–55*	*9 Years* *1956–64*
Chemical shipments	$14.4	$26.9
GNP	316	511

60

This gives us two equations to solve for a and b in the form:

Chemical industry shipments = a(GNP) + b

I. $26.9 = a(511) + b$
II. $14.4 = a(316) + b$

$12.5 = a(195)$ by subtracting equation II from equation I.

$$a = \frac{12.5}{195} = .0641$$

And b can be obtained by substituting in either equation:

I. $26.9 = .0641(511) + b$
II. $14.4 = .0641(316) + b$
I. $b = 26.9 - .0641(511) = -5.9$
II. $b = 14.4 - .0641(316) = -5.9$

The final equation shown is:

Chemical shipments ($ billions) =
.0641 (GNP, $ billions) −5.9.

This shortcut method of using two average points gives results as useful as those derived from the conventionally applied, more tedious, least-squares statistical method.

In some cases, the best form of equation is one that is expressed in logarithms:

Log $Y = a(\log X) + b$,
where:

Y = dependent variable
X = independent variable.

This is a linear equation in log form that can be solved in the same way described above. The arithmetic form of the log equation is:

$Y = cX^{a}$,

where:

   Log c = b.

A time trend can be determined by the semilog equation:

   $Y = aX^T$

or:

   $\text{Log } Y = T(\log X) + \log a,$

where:

   Y = dependent variable
   T = number of years elapsed
   X = growth rate.

For example, when X = 1.05, the growth rate is 5 percent per year.

   Where there is more than one variable, a cross-section type of analysis can be used for a quick estimate. For example, let us take a multiple correlation relationship:

> Total consumption of major textile fibers, million lbs. of cotton equivalent = 13.8 (personal consumption expenditures [PCE], $ billions, 1958 dollars), + 112.4 (change in PCE over previous year, $ billions, 1958 dollars) + 1800.

The first step is to arrange the data so that the relationship of fibers to PCE can be seen for each different range of values for the change in PCE. This is shown in Exhibit 13.

   The relationship:

   Fibers = a(PCE) + c

can then be estimated by using averages of each half of the data for the two groups. The average of these a values is a good estimate of the value of a in:

   Fibers = a(PCE) + b(change in PCE) + c.

Once a is known, the net effect of change in PCE and the

Exhibit 13

**Cross-Section Analysis of the Demand for Textile Fibers
as Related to Personal Consumption Expenditures (PCE)
and the Change in PCE from the Previous Year**

Range of Change:	$5–9		$14–18	
Average Change:	$6.8		$16.2	

Year*	PCE $ Billions (1958)	Fibers Million Lbs. Cotton Equivalent	PCE $ Billions (1958)	Fibers Million Lbs. Cotton Equivalent
1949	$217	5,712	—	—
1954	256	6,389	—	—
1955	—	—	$274	7,117
1956	281	6,909	—	—
1957	288	6,771	—	—
1958	—	—	—	—
1959	—	—	307	7,397
1960	316	7,119	—	—
1961	323	7,230	—	—
1962	—	—	339	7,959
1963	—	—	353	8,225

* Data involving Korean War years are omitted.

Exhibit 14

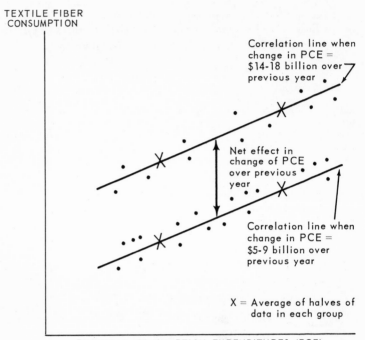

PERSONAL CONSUMPTION EXPENDITURES (PCE)

coefficient b can be determined. The value of c can then be taken as the average value required to give correct values for fibers. This could also be solved graphically as in Exhibit 14.

Estimation of Industrial Company Sales

Shortcut methods of estimating the relationships of company sales to economic indicators can be illustrated by actual data of public companies. In some cases, simple ratios are sufficient.

For example, Park Chemical Co. of Detroit, Michigan, sells metal treating and processing chemicals, used mainly by manufacturers of autos, trucks, tractors, and related items. Therefore, its sales are closely related to automotive production. In fact, between 1954 and 1965 its sales were between $19 and $25 thousand per index point of the FRB production index of motor vehicles and parts, as shown in Exhibit 15. Projecting at this ratio will give a quick forecast of future sales.

About 85 percent of sales at Roberts Consolidated Industries (RCI), City of Industry, California, are carpet installation and adhesive products, and their sales show a strong correlation with U.S. carpet sales. In this case, since RCI has been making acquisitions, we have to subtract the sales of the acquisitions, or retroactively add them back, in order to maintain a true comparison. As shown in Exhibit 16, RCI sales adjusted for acquisitions = .01794 (U.S. broadloom carpet and rug sales) −6.03.

Commercial Filters Corporation (CF) of Lebanon, Indiana, makes filters for heating, air conditioning, chemical processing, aerospace, and food and beverage processing. An analysis shows a close tie-in between sales of Commercial Filters and U.S. purchases of producers' durable equipment for new plants and replacements. This relationship can be used to forecast CF sales, as shown in Exhibit 17.

Donaldson Co. of Minneapolis, Minnesota, makes air cleaners and other accessories primarily for off-road construction, farm, and other equipment. Donaldson sales are closely related to the sales of its customers, which are primarily producers of construction and farm equipment and heavy trucks. But Donaldson is growing faster than its

Exhibit 15

Relationship of Park Chemical Sales to Automobile Production

Year	Park Chemical Sales ($ Millions)	Industrial Production of Motor Vehicles and Parts (1957–59 = 100)	Ratio: Park Sales to FRB Index ($ Thousands Per Index Point)
1954	$2.1	89	$24
1955	2.4	128	19
1956	2.4	103	23
1957	2.4	108	22
1958	2.1	83	25
1959	2.6	109	24
1960	2.6	124	21
1961	2.6	112	23
1962	3.3	134	23
1963	3.7	146	25
1964	3.8	150	25
1965	4.3	177	24

customers, and has also generated sales of about $0.5 million additional every year from new products independent of its present lines. We can adjust for this situation by adding a time trend, that is, by using time as a factor.

The result is: Donaldson sales, $ millions = 4.32 (total sales of construction machinery and equipment, farm machinery and equipment, and heavy duty trucks, $ billions) + 0.5 (year minus 1956) −11.2. This is shown in Exhibit 18.

Exhibit 16

Relationship of RCI Sales to U.S. Carpet Sales

Year	U.S. Broadloom Carpet and Rug Sales ($ Millions)	Roberts Consolidated Industries Sales Adjusted to Comparable Basis from Reported Figures ($ Millions)		Adjusted RCI Sales Estimated from Relationship to U.S. Broadloom Sales*	
		As Reported	As Adjusted**	$ Millions	Actual as Percent of Estimated
1958	$ 559	$ 3.6	$ 4.6	4.0	115%
1959	670	4.8	5.3	6.0	88
1960	667	5.5	5.5	5.9	93
1961	687	6.4	6.4	6.3	103
1962	783	8.4	8.4	8.0	105
1963	883	10.1	10.1	9.8	103
1964	1,035	12.7	12.7	12.5	102
1965	1,156	14.6	14.4	14.7	98
1966	1,245	19.5	15.8	16.3	97

* Based on the following derived equation: RCI Sales = .01794 (U.S. broadloom sales) −$6.03. (All figures in millions of dollars.)
** Adjusted to a comparable basis by adding or subtracting as follows to reported sales: 1958 = $1 million added to adjust retroactively for Anchor and Bechtold acquisitions in 1959 and 1960; 1959 = $0.5 million added to adjust retroactively for Bechtold acquisition in 1960; 1965 = $0.2 million deducted to adjust for partial inclusion of Tavart acquisition; 1966 = $3.7 million deducted from 1966 estimate to adjust for inclusion in part or whole for 1965 and 1966 acquisitions.

Forms of Equations

We have already shown how to handle a second economic factor. The presence of a second factor can be spotted graphically when we seem to have two or more lines of correlation, as shown in Exhibit 14. In the case of the Don-

Exhibit 17

Relationship of CF Sales to U.S. Producers' Durable Equipment Purchases

Year	U.S. Purchases of Producers' Durable Equipment ($ Billions)*	Sales Commercial Filters Corporation Ex Acquisitions ($ Millions) Calculated**	Actual	Actual CF Sales as Percent of Calculated
		Calendar Year Ending 12/31		
1958	$25	$6.7	$6.6	99%
1959	28	7.1	7.9	112
1960	30	7.3	7.5	102
1961	29	7.2	7.4	102
1962	33	7.7	7.4	96
		Fiscal Year Ending 7/31		
1963	34	7.8	7.6	98
1964	37	8.1	8.1	100
1965	43	8.8	8.8	100
1966	49	9.5	9.7	102

* Data for year ending 7/31 estimated by taking average of current and previous years.
** Estimated from historical relationship: Commercial Filter Corporation sales, $ millions = .117 (U.S. purchases of producers' durable equipment, $ billions) + 3.8.

aldson Corporation, a time factor was introduced. Graphically, time factors can be spotted when sales change despite a lack of change in the economic indicator. (See Exhibit 19.) Their effect in the Donaldson case can be quickly calculated by comparing successive values where

Exhibit 18

Donaldson Sales Related to Sales of Principal Customers

Year End 7/31	Construction Machinery and Equipment	Farm Machinery and Equipment	Heavy Duty Trucks	Total Indicator	Actual	Donaldson Sales in $ Millions	
						Calculated from Past Relationship to Indicator*	Actual as Percent of Calculated
1956	$2.2	$1.9	$0.3	$4.4	$ 8.2	$ 7.8	105%
1957	2.1	1.7	0.4	4.2	7.6	7.4	103
1958	1.9	1.7	0.3	3.9	6.9	6.6	105
1959	2.2	2.0	0.3	4.5	10.1	9.7	104
1960	2.2	1.9	0.4	4.5	9.3	10.2	91
1961	2.1	1.8	0.4	4.3	9.5	9.9	96
1962	2.1	2.0	0.4	4.5	11.1	11.2	99
1963	2.4	2.4	0.5	5.3	14.6	15.2	96
1964	2.8	2.7	0.5	6.0	19.3	18.7	103
1965	3.2	3.0	0.6	6.8	21.5	22.6	95

* Based on relationship derived from historical data: Donaldson sales, $ millions = 4.32 (total indicator, $ billions) + 0.5 (year minus 1956) −11.2. Time factor, 0.5 (year minus 1956), indicates that about $0.5 millions of sales are added yearly, independent of sales of principal consuming industries.

the sales change is independent of the indicator change. (See Exhibit 20.)

The change in Donaldson Sales from 1956–57 to 1961, a period of 4.5 years, is $9.5—7.9 million, or $1.6 million, an average of $0.35 million a year. The change from 1959–60 to 1962, a period of 2.5 years, is $11.1—9.7, or $1.4 million, an average of $0.56 million a year. Thus we estimate the average increase in sales to be about $0.5 million per year, even when there is no change in sales in customer industries. By eliminating this as a factor, we can then proceed to find the basic relationship between Donaldson sales and customer industry sales. Taking the data for Donaldson sales, we subtract from each yearly value the amount $0.5 (year −1956), 1956 being the first year for which we have data, and then graphically or otherwise relate the remainder to the sales of Donaldson's customer industries. Graphing the data also allows us to decide

Exhibit 19

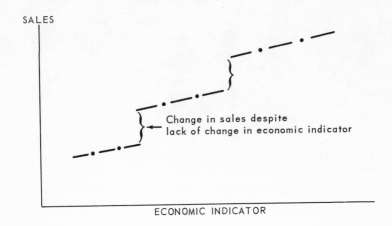

SALES

Change in sales despite
lack of change in economic indicator

ECONOMIC INDICATOR

Exhibit 20

Year	Sales of Construction and Farm Machinery and Equipment and Heavy Duty Trucks ($ Billions)	Donaldson Co. Sales ($ Millions)
1956	4.4	8.2
1957	4.2	7.6
Average 1956–57	4.3	7.9
1961	4.3	9.5
1959	4.5	10.1
1960	4.5	9.3
Average 1959–60	4.5	9.7
1962	4.5	11.1

Exhibit 21

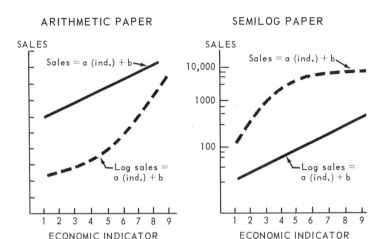

whether we have an arithmetic or logarithmic relationship, as shown in Exhibit 21. Or we can estimate the form of the relationship by looking at the numbers:

1. Increases in sales divided by increases in the economic indicator—
    Sales = a(indicator) + b.
2. Percent increases in sales divided by absolute increases in the economic indicator—
    Log sales = a(indicator) + b.
3. Percent increases in sales divided by percent increases in the economic indicator—
    Log sales = a(log indicator) + b.
    This will give a straight line when graphed on log-log paper.

Time Trends

Correlations to economic indicators cannot always be used; in many cases of fast-growth products, time is the only useful factor in measuring growth. For example, the use of industrial gases has been growing very rapidly—much more rapidly than the economy—because of their applications in new steel processes, aerospace, and food preservation. From 1947 to 1964, sales increased by an average of 8.25 percent per year. This can be measured by relating sales to time:

Industrial gases $= a(\text{growth rate})^{\text{time}}$

or:

Log industrial gases $= \log a + \text{time}(\log \text{growth rate})$.
When the equation is solved, the growth rate is 1.0825, or 8.25 percent per year, as shown in Exhibit 22.

End-Use Analysis

In some cases, products of a company do not lend themselves to correlation with indicators for which forecasts are readily obtainable; or such relations cannot be found; or historical data are not available. In these cases, the end-use method can be used. Total company sales are broken down into small sectors, and each forecast is made individually by standard numerical techniques, judgment, or, if necessary, educated guesses.

For example, Fischer & Porter Co. of Warminster, Pennsylvania, with sales of about $50 million a year, has a product mix for which historical data are not readily available. Educated guesses may be the only way of estimating overall sales growth, as shown in Exhibit 23.

For VSI Corp. of Pasadena, California, with the same

Exhibit 22

Relationship of Industrial Gases to Time

Year	Industrial Gases Shipments Actual ($ Millions)	Industrial Gases Shipments Calculated* ($ Millions)	Industrial Gases Shipments, Actual as Percent of Calculated**
1947	$114	$120	95%
1948	N.A.	130	—
1949	129	141	91
1950	142	152	93
1951	177	165	107
1952	195	179	109
1953	216	193	112
1954	201	200	100
1955	224	227	99
1956	241	245	98
1957	260	265	98
1958	277	287	97
1959	315	311	101
1960	344	337	102
1961	362	364	99
1962	382	394	97
1963	425	427	99
1964	503	462	109

* Log(industrial gases) = .0344(year − 1947) + 2.2307, or industrial gases = 120(1.0825) (year − 1947), indicating a growth rate of 8.25% per year.
** Average error = 4%.

$50 million a year in sales, there are also few historical statistics, and the potentials of sectors have to be guessed at. (See Exhibit 24.)

Summary

Shortcut and simple forecasting procedures that require little time and equipment can be used for quick es-

Exhibit 23

Product Group	Share of Fischer & Porter Sales	"Guesstimated" Growth in World Markets, 1965/1975, Percent Per Year
Process instrumentation	60%	10%
Water treatment equipment	18	5
Digital equipment	10	12
Laboratory and industrial glass	8	8
Castings, fiberglass	4	10
Total	100%	9%*

* Average weighted by shares of total sales.

Exhibit 24

Projection of VSI Corp. Domestic Sales Assuming Constant Share of U.S. Market

	Share of VSI Sales	Growth Rate Total U.S. Consumption
Precision fasteners	40%	4%
Plastic mold bases	35	10–15
Door knobs	12	4
Industrial fasteners	5	6
Tape recorder heads	4	7
Metal forming	4	7
Total	100%	6½–8%*

* Weighted average.

timates. Such shortcuts can be used to relate industrial product demand to economic indicators, and do not indicate a lack of sophistication or scientific methodology, but only a lack of time or availability of equipment. But it is important to remember that the analyst can use these techniques successfully only if he takes a scientific approach to his problems.

4

Forecasting the Economy

ANY forecast of the demand for a specific product must almost always be linked to a forecast of the state of the economy, as well as to other independent demand factors that are discovered in an analysis. Most practical forecasters do not make their own forecasts of the economy, relying on others for this step. Each forecaster should be in a position to work closely with specialists in such work, and should be able to understand their methods and to modify their forecasts if it is necessary or desirable to do so.

The methods used in forecasting the state of the economy are similar in many ways to the methods used in forecasting product demand. From one point of view, the forecasting of the economy is a procedure for forecasting the sum of many product demands, so that all the methods used in product demand forecasting can be used in forecasting the state of the economy, along with other methods. Certainly no one method should be solely relied on if time and money are available for using others. Some methods are better for the short-range picture, others for the long-range picture, and still others for the immediate picture. Some of the specific methods that are used frequently for estimating the future state of the economy include

1. Methods based on single or exclusive causes.
2. Trends and cycles.
3. Hunches and tips.
4. Historical analogy.
5. Chart reading.
6. Leading series.
7. Surveys.
8. Sector analysis.
9. Economic models.

The last four methods are probably the most important methods used by economists today.

Leading Series

Economists use a large number of economic indicators of all different types. The main problem in forecasting is to find the one that is pertinent and appropriate to the problem at hand. The National Bureau of Economic Research has done a great deal of work in trying to identify series of data that "lead" or change their direction before the general economy, and that can therefore be used to indicate a change in the direction of the economy some time ahead. Some sophisticated techniques have been developed, such as the combining of many series to get "diffusion" indices that take advantage of the feeling that "there is safety in numbers." This type of analysis is useful in finding short-term fluctuations, and in indicating turning points in the economy. It is apparently a very sensitive method, and may turn out to be one of the few available for this purpose. On the other hand, it does not shed any light on the forthcoming quantitative level of the economy, and indicates turning points only a few months ahead of time. Often the available data are hard to interpret, and the lead-lag time is by no means fixed, but quite variable.

Surveys

Surveys are carried out to gather data from business-men, salesmen, consumers, purchasing agents, and the like, in order to get their opinions on the business trend, to see what their purchasing or investment intentions are, and to gather the data required to prepare forecasts of the economy by other methods. Surveys are the only way to gain information on intentions, and in some cases are the best —or only—way of forecasting such matters as new capital investment by business. However, the opinions gathered by surveys are always "tentative" in that they represent forecasts of intentions that are not always carried out. The opinions of those surveyed are usually based on some implicit forecast of their own. Furthermore, extensive surveys of this type have been carried out during sound business conditions for about twenty years, but we have little experience with or knowledge of their results during business downtrends.

Sector Analysis

This type of analysis centers around the gross national product (GNP), an estimate of the total output of goods and services in the United States. A recent U.S. government study that shows in some detail the method of estimating gross national product by sector analysis will be described later in this chapter. Data on this business indicator and its principal components are available on a yearly basis for the last 50 years, although revisions are still appearing and the most recent data are the most reliable, with data prior to 1929 very weak. Unfortunately, certain types of data that would be very helpful are not available in sufficient quantities—data on changes in income distribution, for example, are scanty.

In the method of sector analysis, the economy is broken down into key sectors on both the income (national income), and product (gross national product) sides. These sectors include construction, consumer durables, inventories, government, and corporate profits. Each sector is analyzed by various methods such as detailed analysis and correlation with other sectors, and a summary is made to obtain gross national product, national income, and employment. These overall measures are then reconciled and coordinated. Thus estimates are obtained not only of the total figures but also of their individual components. This breakdown is valuable, because an individual component such as personal consumption expenditures may be a better indicator of changes in the demand for a certain commodity than a total overall measure of the economy such as GNP would be.

There are many advantages to the method of sector analysis. There is no heavy reliance on any one factor. Extensive published data and estimates are available. The procedure deemphasizes the short run, and eliminates preoccupation with short-term problems. Forcing thorough penetration and analysis, it catches the aggregate effect of small sector changes. The available evidence indicates that this procedure yields good forecasts, especially for one year ahead. Certainly, it forces the forecaster to reconcile the income, product, and employment aspects of the economy, leading to an organized consistency (of course, the forecaster can be consistently wrong as well as consistently right). The procedure does call attention to gaps in information, and provides a framework for all types of information and data, including psychological and unmeasurable data. The procedure is very flexible, but produces pinpoint answers. If they are wrong, the wrong assumptions and judgments that led to them can usually be traced.

The method also has certain disadvantages, especially if it is not used by trained analysts. For example, some analysts neglect the interdependence of the relevant sectors by using published estimates independently for the various sectors without reconciling them for consistency. A complete sector analysis requires a great deal of work that is often difficult to spell out in detail on paper. Some analysts claim that the procedure has a built-in pessimistic bias, because it appears easier to see the prospective declines than the prospective rises. At the same time, the process is slow and laborious, and certainly not an easy one-man job if any degree of speed is required. The voluminous data necessary may be slow in becoming available, although, fortunately, the speed of availability is increasing. For this last reason, and for other reasons, sector analysis is a poor method for short-term forecasting and for indicating turning points. And because of the bulk of the figures involved, it gives a false sense of precision to the completed analysis. In addition, there are a large number of assumptions and judgments required, the correctness of which will depend upon the skill and luck of the analyst.

Some analysts prefer to center their sector analysis procedure around the Federal Reserve Board index of industrial production. The typical procedure is to break down the index into its industry components and have each of these analyzed separately by an expert in the particular industry. This procedure fails to interrelate the sectors properly, and leaves the job to the analyst, who is not primarily concerned with the sector forecasts and who must force the sector forecasts into a consistent relation. Eventually, construction of input-output models may aid the analyst in such reconciliation and in sector analysis oriented around the FRB production indices.

From a practical viewpoint at this time, the GNP method has the advantage of common usage, since most published forecasts relating to the economy are in terms of the GNP and its components. The analyst working with GNP has a great deal of material available that will contribute to his analysis and enable him to check his findings against those of other experts. This is less true of the FRB indices of industrial production.

Economic Models

The technique of using economic models, often referred to as model building or econometric analysis, is a procedure for constructing a comprehensive, schematic, mathematical statement of the economic situation in a set of integrated equations that can be solved simultaneously. This method has the advantage of quantifying projections for broad areas of economic activity on the basis of assumptions that can be varied. If the forecast is wrong, the wrong assumptions and judgments can be traced. The method also produces pinpoint answers, and the mathematical equations can be treated statistically. It is a method of neatly organizing a great deal of complex past and present data.

The method has many disadvantages. It assumes that the past relationships between the variables are correctly measured, significant, and largely fixed over time, and that they will hold in the future. The weaknesses inherent in assuming such stabilities have already been demonstrated. The method also requires assumptions of values of the exogenous variables—that is, the variables determined outside the system of equations. In practice, the method has not performed too well. Its failure may be partially due to the complicated mathematical computations and the high degree of skill involved. It may also be due to the fact that the method deals only with broad aggregates generally, and has no place for psychological or other unmeasurable factors. Actually, even a complicated mathematical model may be too simple to describe the economy adequately, especially as a closed rather than an open system. If anything, the method is overprecise, using a technique more exact than the data on which the whole analysis is based. Continual progress is being made in developing sound models.

Other Methods

The other methods listed previously all have serious weaknesses, but it is not hard to find economic analysts who put a great deal of faith in them. Some analysts use methods based on single or exclusive causes, putting their faith in sunspots, weather, or perhaps changes in the quantity of money in circulation. Other analysts work with trends and cycles, putting their faith in the existence of regular periodic rhythms. Whether such periodicities exist is questionable. Some statisticians have pointed out that the usual smoothing-out processes that are used, such as the method of moving averages, will show regular wavelike movements even when applied to random series. Some analysts put their faith in hunches and tips; often their background of experience warrants this. Others use historical analogy and attempt to relate the future to some similar past situation. Many spend a great deal of time constructing charts and carefully looking for certain shapes that they claim are a clue to the future. However, most analysts put their faith in hard work, and, while they would like to find a simple, magic formula for the economic future, put this search secondary to turning out balanced, integrated, and consistent economic forecasts.

The forecasting of population and labor force is essential to forecasting the economy and the demand for commodities. Such forecasts can be made by detailed consideration of the components of life expectancy and population changes such as birthrate and immigration. Other factors in determining the labor force are age-group composition of the population, work-life expectancy, and trends in sex composition of the labor force. This type of detailed analysis is more valuable than simple overall trend projection, both in guaranteeing accuracy of results and in yielding meaningful component breakdowns in many types of forecasts.

Many books and articles have been written recently to deal with the details of forecasting the economy by a wide range of methods, and with the difficulties and problems involved in these methods. All agree that it is advisable to use as many of the avaliable methods as are practicable. Certainly, an appraisal of the overall outlook is the first step toward preparing a good commodity forecast, and its importance cannot be overemphasized.

The product analyst, whether or not he is in a position to do his own forecasting of the economy, can obtain such forecasts from many sources; such sources include outside consulting firms, his own economic departments, and published forecasts originating in government agencies, trade associations, private firms, banks, brokers, newspapers, and magazines. He can then utilize these forecasts alone or use them to check his own forecasts.

Forecasting the U.S. Economy by Sector Analysis

In most work involving forecasting of product demand, the procedure is to relate the product demand to an economic indicator. The indicator generally used is the GNP (the total output of goods and services) or one of its components. It is beneficial for the forecaster to understand how economists forecast the GNP and its components, even though he may never do such a forecast himself, relying instead on outside sources.

The most widely used procedure, sector analysis, is described in a recent government pamphlet entitled "U.S. Economic Growth to 1975: Potentials and Problems," a study prepared for the Subcommittee on Economic Progress of The Joint Economic Committee, Congress of the United States (U.S. Government Printing Office, Washington, 1966, $.25). Sector analysis involves detailed consideration of each part of the GNP and its complement, national income (the sum of the receipts of the factors of production). The following is a simplified summary of the pamphlet.

Exhibits 25–27 show the forecasts for 1970 and 1975, compared with 1965 actual; note that some sector values differ slightly from table to table because of rounding. Simply described, the projections were made as follows:

Exhibit 25

Projections of Gross National Product with Major Components Adjusted to Illustrate an Equilibrium Full-Employment Position

Billions of Current Dollars
At 4 Percent Unemployment Level

	$ Billions		
	Actual	Projected	
	1965	1970	1975
Gross National Product	$682	$920	$1205
Personal consumption expenditures	432	583	754
Durable goods	66	88	113
Nondurable goods	191	241	293
Services	175	254	348
Gross private domestic investment	107	138	184
Nonresidential fixed investment	70	85	106
Residential structures	28	45	66
Change in business inventories	9	8	12
Net exports of goods and services	7	9	12
Exports	39	51	66
(Imports)	(32)	(42)	(54)
Government purchases of goods and services	136	190	255
Federal	67	79	93
State and local	69	111	162

( ) Negative value to be subtracted.

First, certain assumptions were made to estimate the future GNP.

   1. The war in Vietnam will be ended or reduced to allow some reductions in war expenditures.

Exhibit 26

Relationship of Gross National Product to National Income and Personal Income

Billions of Current Dollars

	$ Billions		
	Actual	Projected	
	1965	1970	1975
Gross national product	$682	$920	$1205
Less: (Capital consumption allowances)	(60)	(77)	(96)
(Indirect business tax and nontax liability)	(63)	(81)	(108)
(Business transfer payments)	(3)	(3)	(4)
Statistical discrepancy	2	—	—
Plus: Subsidies, Less: (Current surplus of government enterprises)	1	1	neg
Equals: National income	559	760	997
Less: (Corporate profits and inventory valuation adjustment)	(74)	(97)	(118)
(Contributions for social insurance)	(29)	(48)	(67)
Plus: Government transfer payments to persons	37	61	83
Interest paid by government (net) and consumers	20	28	37
Dividends	19	24	30
Business transfer payments	3	3	4
Equals: Personal income	535	731	966
Less: Personal tax and nontax payments	(66)	(97)	(142)
Equals: Disposable personal income	469	634	824
Less: (Personal consumption expenditures)	(431)	(584)	(754)
Less: (Other personal outlays)	(12)	(17)	(24)
Equals: Personal savings	26	33	46

neg Negligible.
( ) Negative value to be substracted.

Exhibit 27

National Income

Billions of Current Dollars

| | $ Billions | | |
| | Actual | Projected | |
	1965	1970	1975
National Income	$559	$760	$ 997
Compensation of employees	393	547	735
Wages and salaries	358	493	662
Private	289	392	520
Government	69	101	142
Supplement to wages and salaries	35	54	73
Private	29	45	61
Government	6	9	12
Proprietors' income	56	65	75
Business and professional	41	50	60
Farm	15	15	15
Rental income of persons	18	20	22
Corporate profits after inventory adjustment	74	97	118
Profits before tax°	76	100	121
Inventory valuation adjustment	(2)	(3)	(3)
Net interest	18	31	47
° Profits before tax	76	100	121
Less: (Taxes)	(31)	(42)	(51)
Profits after tax	45	58	70
Less: (Dividends)	(19)	(24)	(30)
Retained profits	26	34	40

( ) Negative value to be subtracted.

2. The unemployment rate will be 4 percent (versus 4.6 percent in 1965 and 3.8 percent in 1966).
3. The output per man-hour in the private sector will increase 3 percent per year and 2.6 percent per year overall.
4. The labor force will grow to 86 million in 1970 and 94 million in 1975.
5. The armed forces will average 2.7 million in 1970 (about the same as 1965) and 2.6 million in 1975.
6. Average weekly hours will decline ½ hour 1967 to 1970 and another ½ hour 1970 to 1975 (comparable to the 1920s).
7. Overall prices as measured by the GNP deflator will grow 1.5 percent per year (as from 1959 to early 1965).
8. Wage rates, private and public, will rise to cover both the productivity gain (2.6 percent per year per man-hour) and consumer price rises, so that wages as a percent of GNP will be about the same from 1965 to 1975.
9. Personal savings will be about 5 percent to 5.5 percent of disposable personal income (5.5 percent in 1965).
10. Total labor supply will grow about 1.8 percent per year (versus 1.3 percent from 1948 to 1964), reflecting increased population growth.

Therefore, the growth in GNP will be the product of the growth in labor supply, output per man-hour, weekly hours, and prices (after adjustment for unemployment).

The growth factors per year were:

- Labor supply employed   1.8%
- Output per man-hour   2.6%

- Decrease in weekly hours   (0.3)%
- Prices   1.5%

The change per year in GNP in constant dollars = (1.018) (1.026) (0.997) = 1.041, representing a constant dollar GNP change of 4.1 percent per year before adjustment for changes in unemployment rates. With price increase added, the result was 5.7 percent a year for the annual change in GNP in current dollars. The next step was to estimate the various components of the GNP shown in Exhibit 25.

Gross National Product (Exhibit 25)

Personal consumption expenditures. Personal consumption expenditures were estimated by subtracting personal savings from disposable personal income. Disposable personal income was estimated from national income and personal income. Savings were assumed to be 5% to 5.5% of disposable personal income. (The average rate for 1961 to 1965 is 5.5%. It tends to change with the employment rate). The method of estimating national income, personal income, and disposable personal income will be described later in this chapter.

Components of personal consumption expenditures were estimated as follows:

- Durable goods. A relatively high proportion of disposable personal income.
- Nondurable goods. Extension of the trend of the ratio to disposable personal income.
- The residual. The projected ratios to disposable personal income look reasonable.

For durable goods the projections in current dollars were based on a logarithmic regression to disposable personal income using the high employment years since 1948, except 1955 and 1965.

Gross private domestic investment. Components of gross private domestic investment were estimated as follows:

- Residential structures. Ratio to real GNP using postwar data.
- Change in nonfarm business inventories. Ratio to real GNP. It was assumed that farm inventory changes would be negligible.
- Nonresidential fixed investment. The first estimate was a residual one. This gave a figure with too high a ratio to the GNP. There has been a long-term downward trend in this ratio since 1929. The final estimate is reduced from the first residual estimate.

Net exports of goods and services. In estimating net exports, the following relationships were considered:

- Merchandise exports $(58\$) = -2.090 + 0.198$ (GNP abroad) $+ 0.238$ (merchandise imports in the preceding year). This was estimated from the data of 1953 to 1965, except 1956 and 1957.
- Service exports $(58\$)$ based on continuation of the 1953–1965 trend.
- Merchandise imports $= 0.158 + 0.0295$ (GNP), using 1948 to 1965 data.
- Service imports $= -2.688 + 0.0224$ (disposable personal income), based on 1953 to 1965 data.
- Military expenditures $=$ arbitrary estimate assumed close to 1965 rate.

The "GNP abroad" is a special series of GNP data for OECD countries, Canada, and Japan, weighted by U.S. exports to those countries in 1964. The growth rate of "GNP abroad" was assumed to be 4.8% per year.

Government purchases of goods and services. In the estimate of government expenditures, the following were considered:

- Federal purchases. Compensation per employee increased to match private productivity and consumer price rises. Other purchases held constant in real prices, with price increase of 1.5% per year.
- State and local purchases = −29.30 + 0.1796 (national income). Based on data of 1952 to 1965, except 1954, 1958, and 1961.

A moderate rise in federal civilian employment was assumed. The first estimate was raised to reflect utilization of part of the federal surplus. The final estimate was larger than the first by 4% for 1970 and 8% for 1975. Further details are given in the discussion of government compensation below.

Prices. Price series for specific sectors were projected by the logarithmic relationship of the sector price to the overall GNP price level. The relationships were generally based on 1957 to 1965. In most cases the correlation was quite high.

Deriving National Income (Exhibit 26)

Capital consumption allowances (depreciation).

- Corporate = 1.44 + 0.0512(GNP), based on 1962–1965 data. The year 1962 was the first for liberalized depreciation allowances.

- Noncorporate = trend from 1960 to 1965.

Indirect business taxes.

- Federal = 1.12 + 0.024 (GNP adjusted for tax cuts enacted) based on 1955 to first-half 1965 data. Data were adjusted to eliminate nuisance taxes.
- State and local property taxes (as log) = 0.353 + 0.793 (log state and local public education wages and salaries) based on 1950–1965 data. Education wages and salaries = (number of 5- to 21-year-olds) (average expenditure for each) projected as a trend. All other indirect business taxes based on relationship with GNP for recent years.

Business transfer payments.

- Corporate projected by 1955–1965 trend, except 1962.
- Noncorporate projected by 1955–1965 trend.

Subsidies projected by trend.

- Federal: 1961–1965 data, except 1963.
- State and local: 1959–1965 data.

Deriving Personal Consumption Expenditures (Exhibit 26)

Methods of estimating components of national income will be discussed in the explanation of Exhibit 27 below.

Contributions for social insurance. Relationship to taxable wages and salaries adjusted for taxes.

Government transfer payments. To persons in United States:

- Number of beneficiaries. Old-age and survivors, insurance by trend; unemployment insurance by relationship to unemployment in high employment years; others by trend.
- Increase in benefits. Judgment based on projections of Health, Education, and Welfare and other agencies involved.

To foreigners: Trend.

Net interest paid by government. Projected by relationship to gross federal debt (assumed to be held at a $335 billion ceiling) and interest rates. A slow rise in interest rates from 1964 is assumed; state and local net interest assumed lower than recent years because of some decline in interest rate.

Personal taxes. Federal = relationship to personal income less transfers for selected quarters of 1964–1966 (when taxes were reduced) as first estimate. State and local (as log) = $-3.574 + 1.727$ (log personal income less transfers), based on 1960–1965 data. Since the first estimate gave a substantial federal surplus, the tax was reduced as described below.

Other personal outlays. Other personal outlays = $-3.44 + 0.022$ (GNP), based on 1955–1963 data. Assumes interest rates will come down. These are outlays other than purchases of goods and services, with interest being the largest factor.

Components of National Income (Exhibit 27)

Private wages and salaries plus proprietors' income. See proprietors' income alone below. Based on change in private productivity (3% per year), employment, hours, and consumer prices.

Private supplements. Relationship to wages and salaries adjusted for taxes.

Government compensation. Compensation per employee increased 4.2% per year. Federal civilian employment in general government assumed to increase by 20,000 per year in 1975. Military = 2.7 million in 1970, 2.6 million in 1965. State and local employment based on regression with total employment and time factor plus additional 70,000 under poverty program.

Proprietors' income. Business and professional = trend for 1960–1965 data; farm = U.S. Department of Agriculture estimates.

Rental income. Trend 1953–1965.

Corporate profits. A residual. Dividends = 5.97 + 0.1415 (cash flow) + 0.336 (year −1960), based on 1955–1965 data. Corporate profit taxes at 1966 effective rates adjusted for future possibilities. Note that cash flow as used here is defined as corporate retained earnings plus capital consumption allowances (depreciation).

Net interest. Extrapolation of recent data using a freehand curve to allow for an assumed decline in interest rates from recent highs.

Adjusting the First Estimate

The first estimate indicated that increased government expenditures or increased personal consumption expenditures would be required to obtain the desired GNP level. Therefore, the first estimate's surplus of federal receipts over expenditures was used both to increase government expenditures and to cut personal taxes. Of the total surplus, 0.5% was allocated to be retained in 1970, and 1% to be retained in 1975. Of the remainder, one-third was used for personal tax cuts, and two-thirds were transferred to state and local governments. The tax reductions (reductions as a percent of personal tax and nontax payments) resulting from the cut were 3.5% for 1970 and 7% for 1975. An alternative to this procedure would be to relate taxes to government expenditures, and estimate the potential surplus in that way.

All these government figures are gone into in some detail in the cited pamphlet. A copy of the federal budget is a useful adjunct to this study; especially recommended is "The Budget in Brief," Executive Office of the President/ Bureau of the Budget (U.S. Government Printing Office, Washington, 1967, $.35).

Alternate Method

An alternate method (not shown in the pamphlet) would be to relate "investment" (private nonresidential fixed investment plus government expenditures) to GNP. The investment tends to lead. A relationship that takes the lead into account is:

$$\text{GNP} = a \text{ (investment of current year)} + b \text{ (investment of previous year)} + c$$

This is called the multiplier effect, because a small change in investment results in a change several times larger in GNP.

This method gives the private investment plus government expenditures necessary to support a desired GNP level. Subtracting a reasonable private investment figure gives the required government expenditures. Necessary government receipts can then be calculated to lead to a balanced set of national accounts, that is, GNP and national income statements.

5

An Example of
Simple Model Forecasting

V_{ERY} often, the forecasting relationship cannot be simplified to one equation, and needs to be described by a set of equations. In order to understand the procedure employed to make a preliminary evaluation of such a situation, let us examine a method of forecasting jute prices.

Jute is a bast (inner bark) fiber obtained from various varieties of tall plants that grow well in the humid and fertile soil found in hot and very damp climatic conditions. There are a number of allied fibers that can be substituted for jute, the chief being kenaf, also called mesta. These can be grown under less rigorous conditions, in hot and tropical or subtropical zones, and in a wider variety of soil. Kenaf is shorter and coarser than jute, but otherwise very similar. The finest kenaf is used alone; other grades are mixed with jute.

The world's chief jute and kenaf growing areas are in Pakistan and India, and in nearby lands such as Nepal, Thailand, and Burma. Important secondary sources are China, Formosa, and Brazil.

In major producing areas, jute is grown as a cash crop by farmers, much of whose main crop, rice, is produced for their own consumption. The acreage of jute planted is determined both by the price of jute, especially in relation to that of rice, and by the extent of available food supplies. Kenaf, however, is grown in rotation with other crops. It can be grown in less fertile soil than jute, and does not compete as directly as jute does with the growing of staple foodstuffs.

Unfortunately, the jute yield per acre is quite variable, since it is extremely dependent on weather and flooding conditions. However, the average world yield is relatively stable in comparison with yield changes in specific areas. The whole analysis for forecasting purposes is broken down into long- and short-term observations.

Long-term observations. For the most part, the demand for jute is determined independently of price, since in most uses jute is a small part of the total product value, and substitution cannot be quickly made. The price of jute before planting generally determines the amount planted. Thus, on the average, the amount planted corresponds to the demand, although a wide cycle of alternating shortages and surpluses is generated. In the long term, on a three-year average basis, price tends to be related to total demand. The greater the demand, the higher the price.

Short-term observations. A surplus or deficit in production, as compared with demand, results in a change in inventories. The change in February price from year to year is directly related to the inventory change from year to year. The price in February preceding planting of jute determines acreage planted. Weather and other uncontrollable factors affect yield and determine output in the fall. Since, on the average, yield for a set of growing areas has a fairly limited range from year to year, the February price is roughly related to the annual average price. The surplus or deficit in output versus demand again affects the next year's price, and the cycle goes on indefinitely.

Long-Term Forecasts

In the largest producers, India and Pakistan, raw jute is sown in February and March, and harvested between July and September. The analysis indicates that the planted acreage of jute and allied fibers is highly dependent on the February jute price. The statistics and their derived relationships are shown in Exhibit 28. The results of these relationships are not too far from actual. It should be noted that the February price for the year averages 100% to 108% of the average annual price, on a three-year basis. All statistical relationships were derived graphically without computers; computer analysis would give far better results.

World consumption of jute is expected to grow 1% to 5% per year. Assuming that the 1970 consumption will (on the average) equal output, the question is: What will be the corresponding average price? The forecasts can be derived by

1. Estimating consumption for 1970 by the expected growth rate, and assuming it approximately equal to desired output, to meet demand.
2. Using a range of yields per acre.

Exhibit 28

Relationship of February Jute Price to Acreage of Jute and Allied Fiber Planted

(All Calculations Done by Slide Rule)

Year	February Price Mill Lightnings CIF Dundee £/Ton	World Acreage Planted (Except Russia) (Thousand Acres)		Calculated Acreage (Thousand Acres)	
		Jute	Allied Fibers	Jute*	Allied Fibers**
1955 (a)	£ 109.00	3,583	808	3,550	1,140
1956	88.00	3,368	1,035	3,470	1,050
1957	106.00	3,534	1,058	3,630	1,200
1958	97.00	3,598	1,144	3,550	1,150
1959	90.00	3,331	1,090	3,390	1,050
1960	102.50	3,297	1,308	3,550	1,150
1961	199.00	4,623	1,879	4,470	1,820
1962	127.50	4,130	1,458	3,890	1,380
1963	120.00	4,133	1,605	3,810	1,320
1964	120.00			3,810	1,320
1965	156.00			4,170	1,550
1970 Low	155–200				
1970 High	285–370				

(a) Pakistan acreage restricted by government

* Log jute acreage $= 0.35$ (log jute price) $+ 2.85$.

** Log allied fiber acreage $= 0.69$ (log jute price) $+ 1.68$.

Exhibit 28

(*continued*)

Actual Acreage as Percent of Calculated		Prices		
		3-Year Average £/Ton		
Jute	Allied Fibers	Average Annual Price	Average February Price	February as Percent of Average Price
101%	71%	£ 91.52	£ 98.50	108%
97	98	95.12	101.00	106
97	88	97.10	97.00	100
101	99	97.63	97.66	100
99	104	105.86	96.50	91
93	114	128.56	130.50	102
104	104	135.07	143.00	106
106	106			
108	121	129.83	148.83	114
		155–185	155–200	100–108%
		285–342	285–370	100–108%

3. Deriving February price from the relationships in Exhibit 28.
4. Deriving annual average price by taking February price as 100% to 108% of annual price. (See Exhibit 28.)

Step 3, the derivation of the February price, is done from the relationships shown in Exhibit 28 by converting them as follows:

A. Log (jute acreage) = 0.35 log (February jute price) + 2.85.
B. Log (allied fiber acreage) = 0.69 log (February jute price) + 1.68.

Converting these to exponential form, we get:

C. Jute acreage = (February jute price)$^{0.35}$(708).
D. Allied fiber acreage = (February jute price)$^{0.69}$ (48).

And since:

E. (Jute acreage) (jute yield per acre) + (allied fiber acreage) (allied fiber yield per acre) = output of jute and allied fibers.

combining these, we get:

F. Output of jute and allied fibers = (February jute price)$^{0.35}$(708) (jute yield per acre) + (February jute price)$^{0.69}$ (48) (allied fiber yield per acre).

With:

- Acreage in thousand acres.
- Price in £/long ton CIF Dundee.
- Yield in tons (metric or long) per acre.
- Output in thousand tons (metric or long).

This last equation (F) is one that can be solved only by trial and error, because of its exponential form.

Short-Term Forecasts

The procedure described for long-term forecasts has to make the assumption that production will equal consumption. Actually, in the short-term this is not always true. A suggested method for forecasting jute prices for a year ahead is to use the relationship between prices and stocks. Exhibit 29 shows that: Increase/decrease in average price (£/ton) from previous year = −0.116 (Change in June 30 stocks [thousand tons] from previous year) + 11.8.

The change in stocks can be estimated by estimating the production surplus or deficit as the difference between actual production and average production:

A. Average production in thousand tons = 2,000 + 100 (year −1952).
B. Change in stocks in thousand tons = 0.75 (production surplus/deficit of previous year in thousand tons) + 100,

where the surplus or deficit is actual production less average production. The results are shown in Exhibit 30. Since,

(*Text continued on p. 107*)

Exhibit 29

Price Inventory Relationships

(Average Annual Price to Inventory Change)

Year	Increase/(Decrease) from Previous Year		Calculated by Formula° £/Ton		Actual as Percent of Calculated Price
	Price £/Ton	Stock (Thousand Tons)	Price Change	Price	
1951	7.90	(420)	NA	NA	NA
1952 (a)	£ 64.64	NA	£(28.6)	£148	75%
1953	(66.45)	348	(26.6)	84	102
1954 (b)	(24.50)	331	60.4	146	64
1955 (b)	(4.15)	(170)	31.5	125	72
1956	1.15	65	4.3	94	97
1957	13.75	115	(1.5)	89	118
1958	(8.90)	25	8.9	114	84
1959	(3.25)	120	(2.0)	94	99
1960	36.85	(289)	45.3	138	93
1961	34.50	(166)	31.0	160	102
1962	(51.85)	527	(49.2)	114	98
1963	1.65	92	1.2	113	101
1964	12.45	(84)	21.5	135	93
1965 e		24 (c)	9.0	135°°	
1966 e		81 (c)	2.4	138°°	

(a) Korean War, June 1950 to July 1953, had abnormal effects.
(b) Artificial price restrictions by Pakistan government.
(c) From Exhibit 30.
NA Not available.
  e Estimated.
  ° Price change calculated from equation: Price change = −0.116 (change in stocks) + 11.8.
°° By adding price change to previously calculated value.

104

Exhibit 30

Estimate of Stock Changes Jute and Allied Fibers
(World Except Russia)
Thousand Tons

Previous Year	Production			Current Year	Change in India & Pakistan Jute Stocks		Actual as Percent of Calculated Stock Change
	Actual	Average*	Surplus/ (Deficit) over Average		Actual	Calculated**	
1951	2,275	1,900	375	1952	348	382	91%
1952	2,350	2,000	350	1953	331	362	92
1953	1,644	2,100	(456)	1954	(420)	(244)	172
1954	1,872	2,200	(328)	1955	(170)	(145)	118
1955	2,285	2,300	(15)	1956	65	89	73
1956	2,360	2,400	(40)	1957	115	70	164
1957	2,354	2,500	(146)	1958	25	(10)	NS
1958	2,682	2,600	82	1959	120	161	75
1959	2,504	2,700	(196)	1960	(289)	(48)	600
1960	2,329	2,800	(471)	1961	(166)	(255)	65
1961	3,442	2,900	542	1962	527	510	104
1962	2,948	3,000	(52)	1963	92	61	150
1963	3,120	3,100	20	1964	(84)	115	NS
1964	3,099	3,200	(101)	1965	NA	24	NA
1965	3,275	3,300	(25)	1966	NA	81	NA

* Average production = 2,000 + 100 (Year −1952).
** Change in stocks = 0.75 (production surplus/deficit of previous year) + 100.

NA Not available.
NS Not significant.

Exhibit 31

Estimate of February Jute Prices

Previous Year	Production Surplus/ (Deficit) over Average Thousand Tons	Current Year	Increase/ (Decrease) in February Jute Price over Previous Year £/Ton	Calculated Price Change £/Ton*	Year	February Price £/Ton		As Percent of Calculated Price
						Actual	Calculated	
1956	(40)	1957	£ 18.00	£ 25.7	1956	£ 88.00	£ —	—
1957	(146)	1958	(9.00)	43.4	1957	106.00	114	93%
1958	82	1959	(7.00)	5.4	1958	97.00	149	65
1959	(196)	1960	12.50	51.6	1959	90.00	102	88
1960	(471)	1961	96.50	97.8	1960	102.50	142	73
1961	542	1962	(71.50)	(72.0)	1961	199.00	200	100
1962	(52)	1963	(7.50)	27.7	1962	127.50	127	100
1963	20	1964	0.00	15.7	1963	120.00	155	78
1964	(101)	1965		35.8	1964	120.00	136	89
1965	(25)	1966		23.2	1965		156	
					1966		179	

* Price change = −.167 (production surplus/deficit of previous year) −19.00.

as is shown, the planted acreage depends on the February price, it is of interest to forecast the February jute price, and from that the acreage planted. The method shown in Exhibit 31 is to relate it to the production surplus/deficit of the previous year (see Exhibit 30) as follows:

Increase/decrease in February jute price (£/ton) from previous year = −1.67 (production surplus/deficit of previous year in thousand tons) + 19.00.

This makes it possible to estimate the February price from the previous year's production, and the acreage planted that year from the February price, using the relationship in Exhibit 28. Combined with a yield estimate, this gives an estimate for the current year's output. In addition, as the year progresses, reports on the weather and state of the crop allow modification of the estimate between planting time in February and harvest in the Fall.

About the Author

WILLIAM COPULSKY has been affiliated with W. R. Grace & Co. since 1951, where he is now Director, Commercial Department. He is also a lecturer at the Graduate Division of Baruch College and a director and board member of Electronucleonics Laboratories, Inc.

Mr. Copulsky received his B.A. in Chemistry at New York University; M.B.A., Baruch College; and Ph.D., N.Y.U. Graduate School of Business. He is a member of the American Statistical Association, American Chemical Society, Commercial Chemical Development Association, Chemical Marketing Association, and American Marketing Association. A frequent speaker at American Management Association, Mr. Copulsky is the author of several books and over 30 articles in the fields of marketing and forecasting.